THE
CORONATION STREET
QUIZ BOOK

Graeme Kay & Chris Stacey

D1385613

B◈XTREE

First edition first published in the UK 1990 by
Boxtree Limited
Broadwall House
21 Broadwall
London SE1 9PL

First revised edition published 1994

This edition first published in the UK 1995 by
Boxtree Ltd in association with Granada Television

10 9 8 7 6 5 4 3 2 1

Cover design by Design 23

Printed and bound in Great Britain by
Caledonian International Book Manufacturing Ltd, Glasgow

ISBN: 0 7522 0197 2

CONTENTS

INTRODUCTION

Welcome to the Coronation Street Quiz Book. On December 9th 1995 *Coronation Street* will celebrate 35 years consistently topping the ratings charts, despite intrusions from eighties' 'upstarts' *Brookside* and *EastEnders*. There is no stopping the Street . . .

Eighteen million viewers tune in devotedly to watch every 'cough and sneeze' of the action in this Pickwick Papers-style serial about which the late poet laureate Sir John Betjeman eulogised 'Not a word too many. Not a gesture needless. It is the best writing and acting I could wish to see . . .'.

Consequently, thousands of enthusiasts consider themselves experts on *Coronation Street* folklore. To find out how good your knowledge of the people of Weatherfield is this book has been arranged on three levels.

Section One consists of starter questions for beginners or casual watchers. If you don't know the answers to the multiple choice questions, have a guess and join in the fun!

Section Two is for *Coronation Street* addicts. So you think you know your Street? Well let's see how much you really do know about the A to Z of Ena Sharples and Co.

If you score well on Sections One and Two, you should relish the challenge of **Section Three**, *Coronation Street* Masterclass. This section boasts really tough quizzes that even the very sharpest of you will find tough to cope with, without the answers at hand!

If you're tackling this quiz book in company with family or friends and you're keeping score, the last quiz of this section – Champion's Tie Breaker – should sort out who is the undisputed champion of your group. Good luck!

SECTION ONE:
Coronation Street

STARTERS

People . . .

1. Who invented *Coronation Street*?
   (a) Harry Kershaw. (b) Stuart Latham. (c) Tony Warren.
   (d) Roald Dahl.

2. How many famous ladies drank milk stout in the Snug?
   (a) Two. (b) Three. (c) Four.

3. Who was the first landlord of The Rover's Return?
   (a) Len Fairclough. (b) Ken Barlow. (c) Jack Walker.
   (d) Jack Archer.

4. What was Elsie Tanner's son called?
   (a) Dave. (b) Stan. (c) Dennis. (d) Adrian.

5. Which brewery owns The Rover's Return?
   (a) Smiths. (b) Greens. (c) Newton and Ridley.
   (d) Ind Coope.

6. What was Minnie Caldwell's favourite lodger called?
   (a) Eddie Yeats. (b) Billy Walker. (c) Sonny Jim.
   (d) Dirty Den.

7. Which barmaid did Harry Hewitt marry?
   (a) Bet Lynch. (b) Sheila Birtles. (c) Concepta Riley.
   (d) Dolly Skilbeck.

8. Who was the Street's first lollipop man?
   (a) Percy Sugden. (b) Leonard Swindley.
   (c) Albert Tatlock. (d) Walter Gabriel.

9. How did Ernest Bishop (Emily's first husband) die in 1978?
   (a) Natural causes. (b) Heart attack.
   (c) Gunshot wounds. (b) Old age.

10. What was Elsie Tanner's favourite tipple?
    (a) Vodka and Tonic. (b) Gin and tonic.
    (c) Whisky and dry. (d) Ginger beer.

Answers on p. 100

. . . *and Places*

1. Where is *Coronation Street* set?
   (a) Chesterfield. (b) Huddersfield. (c) Weatherfield.
   (d) Mansfield.

2. What is the name of Rita Fairclough's shop?
   (a) Rita's Place. (b) The Kabin. (c) Fairclough's Store.
   (d) Weatherfield Newsagents.

3. Where was Tony Warren born?
   (a) Salford. (b) Winsford. (c) Manchester. (d) Ashford.

4. Where did Ena Sharples go to live?
   (a) St Annes on Sea. (b) Clacton on Sea. (c) St Bees.
   (d) St Albans.

5. Which country did Ken Barlow's brother David emigrate
   to in 1968?
   (a) New Zealand. (b) Canada. (c) South Africa.
   (d) Australia.

6. Where did Steve and Elsie Tanner spend their
   honeymoon?
   (a) Blackpool. (b) Majorca. (c) Lisbon. (d) America.

7. Where did Stan Ogden's fancy woman live?
   (a) Rosamund Street. (b) Inkerman Street.
   (c) Viaduct Street. (d) The Flying Horse.

8. Which school did Bet Lynch go to?
   (a) Bessie Street. (b) Weatherfield Girls.
   (c) Salford Juniors. (d) Manchester High.

9. Where did Linda Cheveski return from in 1966?
   (a) Canada. (b) Australia. (c) America. (d) Alaska.

10. On which front did Albert Tatlock serve in 1916?
    (a) The Russian Front. (b) The Somme.
    (c) The White Cliffs of Dover.

Answers on p. 100

First Cast

1. What was Violet Carson's former famous BBC role?

   (a) Wilfred Pickle's pianist. (b) Gilbert Harding's PA.
   (c) Tommy Handley's gag writer.

2. Which comedienne played Elsie Lappin in Episode One?

   (a) Ethell Revnell. (b) Beryl Reid. (c) Hilda Baker.
   (d) Maudie Edwards.

3. Who was the first regular cast member to die?

   (a) Frank Pemberton. (b) Arthur Leslie.
   (c) Lynne Carol. (d) Betty Alberge.

4. Who played Ena Sharples' best chum Minnie Caldwell?

   (a) Doris Speed. (b) Margot Bryant. (c) Noel Dyson.
   (d) Peggy Mount.

5. Which early Street actress is married to James Bolam?

   (a) Sandra Gough. (b) Christine Hargreaves.
   (c) Susan Jamieson. (d) Anne Cunningham.

6. What nationality was actor Ernst Walder who played
   Ivan Cheveski?

   (a) Polish. (b) German. (c) Austrian.

7. Where was Pat Phoenix born?

   (a) Ireland. (b) Manchester. (c) Blackpool.

8. Who played Dennis Tanner's girlfriend – the snake-
   charming stripper?

   (a) Angela Lansbury. (b) Angela Douglas.
   (c) Angela Crowe. (d) Angela Rippon.

9. Which famous radio series was Jack Howarth in before
   he became Albert Tatlock?

   (a) *Dick Barton – Special Agent*. (b) *The Archers*.
   (c) *Mrs Dale's Diary*.

10. Which fellow Street actor did Doreen Keogh marry?

    (a) Arthur Lowe. (b) Peter Adamson. (c) Ivan Beavis.
    (d) Ken Farrington.

Answers on p. 100

Star Quotes

Which celebrity or critic said this about *Coronation Street*?

1. 'The programme is doomed from the outset with its grim scene of terraced houses and smoking chimneys.'
   (a) Janet Street Porter. (b) Ken Irwin. (c) Robin Day.

2. 'There was life before *Coronation Street*, but it didn't add up to much.'
   (a) John Osborne. (b) Vera Lynn. (c) Russell Harty.

3. 'Tell me, where is the real Coronation Street?'
   (a) The Queen. (b) Mrs Thatcher. (c) Cecil Parkinson.

4. 'I must still make clear my personal preference for *Coronation Street*.'
   (a) Terry Wogan. (b) Neil Kinnock. (c) Harold Wilson.

5. 'Manchester produces what is to me *Pickwick Papers*. Mondays and Wednesdays, I live for them.'
   (a) John Betjeman. (b) Larry Olivier. (c) Harry Worth.

6. 'A fascinating Freemasonry. A volume of unwritten rules – these are the driving force behind a working class northern street.'
   (a) Willy Russell. (b) Melvyn Bragg. (c) Tony Warren.

7. 'It's what you'd expect from the North. Damned fine Stuff.'
   (a) Cyril Smith. (b) J. B. Priestley. (c) Gracie Fields.

8. 'I've watched the programme go out in Hong Kong with Chinese sub-titles and wonder what they can mean.'
   (a) Violet Carson. (b) Bill Podmore. (c) Pat Phoenix.

9. 'Elsie Tanner is the sexiest woman on TV.'
   (a) Roger Moore. (b) Dirk Bogarde.
   (c) James Callaghan.

10. 'What can I say but congratulations on your two thousandth episode.'
    (a) Ken Irwin. (b) Kenneth Tynan.
    (c) Kenneth Williams.

Answers on p. 100

1. Who died in the Snug over her milk stout?
   (a) Minnie Caldwell. (b) Martha Longhurst.
   (c) Christine Hardman. (d) Annie Walker.

2. Who was trapped under the rubble when the Viaduct collapsed?
   (a) Elsie Tanner. (b) Lucille Hewitt. (c) Rita Fairclough.
   (d) Ena Sharples.

3. Who died under the wheels of a bus?
   (a) Ida Barlow. (b) May Hardman. (c) Hilda Ogden.
   (d) Alice Pickens.

4. Who broke her pelvis in a 1969 coach crash?
   (a) Emily Nugent. (b) Deirdre Hunt. (c) Maggie Clegg.
   (d) Irma Odgen.

5. Whose ex-policeman husband died in 1974?
   (a) Ena Sharples'. (b) Betty Turpin's. (c) Janet Reid's.
   (d) Eunice Nuttal's.

6. Who died under Len Fairclough's van when the jack collapsed?
   (a) Billy Walker. (b) Ernie Bishop. (c) Harry Hewitt.
   (d) Monkey Gibbon.

7. Who confessed to killing Steve Tanner then shot himself?
   (a) Eddie Yeats. (b) Greg Flint. (c) Joe Donnelli.
   (d) Arnold Swain.

8. What was the name of Alf Roberts' first wife who died in hospital?
   (a) Renée. (b) Mary. (c) Irene. (d) Phyllis.

9. Who broke his toe on a council paving stone?
   (a) Jack Walker. (b) Stan Odgen. (c) Albert Tatlock.
   (d) Mike Baldwin.

10. Whose daughter died of a brain tumour?
    (a) Elsie Tanner's. (b) Ena Sharples'.
    (c) Annie Walker's. (d) Betty Turpin's.

Answers on p. 101

Which Year?

In which year did the following *Coronation Street* incidents or events occur?

1. Jerry Booth married Myra Dickinson in:
   (a) 1963. (b) 1968. (c) 1970. (d) 1989.

2. Patricia Phoenix died in:
   (a) 1979. (b) 1981. (c) 1986. (d) 1988.

3. Jean Alexander retired from her Hilda Ogden role in:
   (a) 1975. (b) 1985. (c) 1987. (d) 1988.

4. Ernie Bishop married Emily Nugent in:
   (a) 1965. (b) 1984. (c) 1979. (d) 1971.

5. Valerie Barlow was electrocuted in:
   (a) 1963. (b) 1971. (c) 1958. (d) 1983.

6. The Mike Baldwin, Ken and Deirdre Barlow affair occurred in:
   (a) 1961. (b) 1970. (c) 1983. (d) 1986.

7. Stan and Hilda celebrated their Ruby Wedding in:
   (a) 1983. (b) 1975. (c) 1980. (d) 1987.

8. Mavis Riley married Derek Wilton in:
   (a) 1979. (b) 1986. (c) 1988. (d) 1985.

9. Alan Bradley was jailed for his attack on Rita in:
   (a) 1983. (b) 1989. (c) 1986. (d) 1975.

10. Elsie's daughter Linda emigrated to Montreal in:
    (a) 1985. (b) 1965. (c) 1961. (d) 1970.

Answers on p. 101

Gone, But Not Forgotten

1. Where did Carmel go after she had a nervous breakdown?

2. What did Steph Barnes do to Kevin Webster?

3. What was the name of Brendan Scott's wife?

4. What was Neil Mitchell's profession?

5. How old would Brian Tilsley have been in October 1993?

6. Where did Angie Freeman head for when she left Weatherfield?

7. Where did Amy and Dominic Nelson go to live?

8. What was Colin Barnes' profession?

9. When Jenny Bradley returned to the Street in 1993 she brought her dog with her. What was the dog's name?

10. How old was Lisa Duckworth when she died?

Answers on p. 105

Fleeting Faces

Who were the stars who appeared briefly in the following roles?

1. Elsie Tanner's ageing beau, Harry Payne:
   (a) Max Miller. (b) Max Wall. (c) Roy Hudd.

2. Len Fairclough's son Stanley:
   (a) Ringo Starr. (b) Freddie Garrity.
   (c) Herman of the Hermits. (d) Marty Wilde.

3. Police Constable Willocks who arrested Ena Sharples:
   (a) Terence Stamp. (b) Ronnie Barker.
   (c) Richard Beckinsale. (d) Ronnie Corbett.

4. Ena Sharples' grandson Colin:
   (a) Davey Jones of the Monkees.
   (b) Gerry of Pacemakers fame. (c) Tommy Steele.
   (d) Ricky Livid.

5. Song agent Micky Malone:
   (a) Tommy Tinder. (b) Charlie Chester.
   (c) Bill Maynard.

6. Ken Barlow's graduate girlfriend Elaine Perkins:
   (a) Barbara Windsor. (b) Joanna Lumley.
   (c) Diana Rigg. (d) Liz Fraser.

7. Annie Walker's licensed victuallers friend Nellie Harvey:
   (a) Mollie Sugden. (b) Thora Hird. (c) Hylda Baker.
   (d) Janet Brown.

8. Irma Odgen's boyfriend Ron Jenkins:
   (a) Charles Dance. (b) Kenneth Brannagh.
   (c) Ben Kingsley. (d) Jeremy Irons.

9. Bus conductress Eileen Hughes:
   (a) Julia McKenzie. (b) Prunella Scales.
   (c) Wanda Ventham. (d) Patricia Hodge.

10. Hippie commune leader Robert Croft:
    (a) Martin Shaw. (b) Timothy Dalton.
    (c) Patrick Mower.

Answers on p. 101

Whose Baby?

1. What was the name of the first baby to be born in Coronation Street?

   (a) John Walker. (b) Sally Barlow. (c) Paul Cheveski.

2. Which baby was kidnapped in 1962?

   (a) Christopher Hewitt. (b) Stanley Fairclough.
   (c) Tommy Booth. (d) Paul Tanner.

3. Whose wife gave birth to twins in 1965?

   (a) David Barlow's. (b) Ken Barlow's.
   (c) Harry Hewitt's. (d) Jerry Booth's.

4. Who turned to adoption after a miscarriage in 1967?

   (a) Valerie Barlow. (b) Audrey Fleming.
   (c) Irma Barlow. (d) Jenny Sutton.

5. Who ran off, leaving his wife and baby, in 1978?

   (a) Len Fairclough. (b) Ray Langton. (c) David Barlow.
   (d) Eddie Yeats.

6. Who had a 7lb 2oz baby boy in December 1980?

   (a) Gail Tilsley. (b) Bet Lynch. (c) Deirdre Barlow.

7. Whose illegitimate son was brought up by Maggie Clegg?

   (a) Bet Lynch's. (b) Hilda Ogden's. (c) Betty Turpin's.
   (d) Albert Tatlock's.

8. Whose grandson Darren died in a car crash in Australia?

   (a) Martha Longhurst's. (b) Percy Sugden's.
   (c) Hilda Ogden's. (d) Alf Roberts'.

9. Who had an illegitimate son by ex-Borstal boy Frank Bradley?

   (a) Bet Lynch. (b) Elsie Tanner. (c) Rita Fairclough.

10. What is the name of Nicky Tilsley's little sister?

    (a) Stephanie. (b) Sally Anne. (c) Sarah Louise.

Answers on p. 101

Rogues' Gallery

1. Who played the ex 'tea leaf' that Minnie Caldwell called Sonny Jim?

   (a) Kenneth Cope. (b) Kenneth Williams. (c) Ken Dodd. (d) Ken Platt.

2. Who was caught drinking milk stout and accused of intemperance by Leonard Swindley?

   (a) Annie Walker. (b) Elsie Tanner. (c) Betty Turpin. (d) Ena Sharples.

3. Who got drunk and assaulted a policeman in 1963?

   (a) Eddie Yeats. (b) Albert Tatlock. (c) Dennis Tanner.

4. Who was arrested for driving the wrong way up a one-way street?

   (a) Mavis Riley. (b) Dawn Prescott. (c) Emily Nugent. (d) Gail Tilsley.

5. Who was held captive by an escaped convict in 1968?

   (a) Deirdre Barlow. (b) David Barlow.
   (c) Valerie Barlow. (d) Dilly Barlow.

6. Who appeared in court for shoplifting in 1969?

   (a) Elsie Tanner. (b) Maggie Clegg. (c) Minnie Caldwell. (d) Audrey Fleming.

7. Who bigamously married Emily Bishop in 1980?

   (a) Dave Smith. (b) Arnold Swain. (c) Fred Gee.

8. Which family got fined for not having a TV licence in 1984?

   (a) The Ogdens. (b) The Walkers. (c) The Barlows. (d) The Duckworths.

9. Which Street resident was fined £2 for shoplifting in 1961?

   (a) Frank Barlow. (b) Concepta Riley. (c) Ena Sharples.

10. What happened to the killers of Ernest Bishop in 1978?

    (a) They were never caught. (b) They got probation. (c) They got life imprisonment.

Answers on p. 101

True or False?

1. Lynne Perrie is the sister of comedian Duggie Brown.
   True or false?

2. Elsie Tanner had three husbands.
   True or false?

3. Coronation Street was originally called Florizel Street.
   True or false?

4. Actor Alan Browning was related to Robert Browning the poet.
   True or false?

5. Sue Nicholls, who plays Audrey Roberts, is really the Honourable Susan Harmer-Nicholls.
   True or false?

6. William Roache is the only surviving actor from Episode one.
   True or false?

7. *Coronation Street* has always been at the top of the TV audience ratings.
   True or false?

8. West End theatre impresario Bill Kenwright started out in *Coronation Street*.
   True or false?

9. *Coronation Street* is set in Manchester where Tony Warren was born.
   True or false?

10. Bernard Youens who played Stan Ogden, used to be a velvet-voiced TV announcer.
    True or false?

Answers on p. 102

The Youth Of The Nineties

1. Who was delivery boy for Brendan Scott when he ran the corner shop in 1993?

2. What did Tom Casey give his son Mark for his 21st birthday in 1991?

3. In 1991 where did Tracy Barlow go on a school trip?

4. In the summer of 1990 which country did Jenny Bradley and Flick Khan visit?

5. Name the older man Jenny Bradley fell in love with.

6. Which school does Nicky Platt attend?

7. Name the Nanny from Hell who pursued Martin and Gail during 1992 and 1993.

8. Name the two lads who had a boys' Christmas in Blackpool in 1992.

9. Mike Baldwin pays Mark Redman's fees for attending a private school. What is the name of the school?

10. In 1993 Tracy Barley moved out of No. 1 to live with her boyfriend. What was his name?

Answers on p. 105

Street Speak

What is the meaning of these common *Coronation Street* expressions?

1. Hey up!
   (a) Tea up. (b) Take care. (c) Hello.
   (d) Look who's here!

2. Pie-can.
   (a) Cooking utensil. (b) A fool. (c) Indian bird.
   (d) Tinned pudding.

3. Allus.
   (a) Always. (b) Overall. (c) Machine tool.
   (d) The lot of us.

4. Clemmed.
   (a) Cold. (b) Old. (c) Hungry. (d) Sick.

5. Cludgy.
   (a) Muddy. (b) Foggy. (c) Stream. (d) Outdoor toilet.

6. Flummoxed.
   (a) Puzzled. (b) Tired. (c) Sick. (d) Worn out.

7. Ginnel.
   (a) Mongrel. (b) Alleyway. (c) Steam engine. (d) Needle.

8. Nowty.
   (d) Draughty. (b) Bad tempered. (c) Muggy. (d) Woody.

9. Dropped off't hooks.
   (a) Slipped up. (b) Died. (c) Demoted. (d) Married.

10. Pobs.
    (a) Beans on toast. (b) Mushy peas.
    (c) Bread soaked in warm milk. (d) Bacon bits.

Answers on p. 102

Stars of Song

1. Where did Rita Fairclough make her singing debut?
   (a) The Rover's Return. (b) The Flying Horse.
   (c) The Orinoco Club. (d) Salford Casino.

2. What instrument did Ena Sharples play?
   (a) Violin. (b) Harmonium. (c) Double bass.

3. What was Jack Duckworth's professional stage name?
   (a) Jack O'Casey. (b) Jack the Lad. (c) Vince St Clair.

4. Which actor was a trained classical pianist off set?
   (a) Peter Adamson. (b) Roy Barraclough.
   (c) Stephen Hancock.

5. Which actor plays the ukelele George Formby style?
   (a) Bill Waddington. (b) Michael le Vell. (c) Bill Tarmey.

6. Which actress was a big band singer during the war?
   (a) Doris Speed. (b) Violet Carson. (c) Betty Driver.
   (d) Margot Bryant.

7. Who sang 'We're a Couple of Swells' in a 1984 Street
   talent contest?
   (a) Bet and Deirdre. (b) Vera and Ivy.
   (c) Stan and Hilda. (d) Mavis and Rita.

8. Who was Rita Fairclough's manager before she gave up
   cabaret?
   (a) Jack Duckworth. (b) Alec Gilroy. (c) Brian Tilsley.
   (d) Alan Bradley.

9. Who sang as the Andrew Sisters in the Street's 1972
   Christmas 1940s Show?
   (a) Minnie Caldwell, Martha Longhurst and Ena Sharples.
   (b) Hilda Ogden, Rita Fairclough and Mavis Riley.
   (c) Betty Turpin, Bet Lynch and Norma Ford.

10. Who took in an entire girls' pipe band as lodgers in 1967?
    (a) Lucille Hewitt. (b) Jerry Booth. (c) Sonny Jim.
    (d) Dennis Tanner.

Answers on p. 103

Funny Men!

1. Who was the Street binman who went on to chastise Mrs Pomfrey's dog in *All Creatures Great and Small*?

    (a) Chalkie Whiteley. (b) Rusty Brown.
    (c) Jimmy Green. (d) Red Buttons.

2. What animal did Dennis Tanner keep in his mother's bath?

    (a) An otter. (b) A seal. (c) A sea-lion. (d) A tortoise.

3. How were Jack Duckworth's romantic capers curtailed by his wife in 1989?

    She: (a) stopped his pocket money;
    (b) locked him in the loo; (c) cut up all his trousers.

4. Who did a TV drag act with Les Dawson before he joined the Street cast?

    (a) Roy Barraclough. (b) Kevin Kennedy.
    (c) Chris Quinten.

5. What was Charlie Moffitt's job at the Viaduct Sporting Club in 1964?

    (a) Doorman. (b) Resident comic. (c) Warm-up man.

6. What did fat man Eddie Yeats take up as a hobby in 1982?

    (a) Palmistry. (b) Clog dancing. (c) CB radio.

7. Who took an exotic dancer for a housekeeper in 1989?

    (a) Ken Barlow. (b) Percy Sugden. (c) Alec Gilroy.
    (d) Mike Baldwin.

8. Who wanted to mate his cock budgie with Mavis Riley's hen in 1983?

    (a) Albert Tatlock. (b) Percy Sugden. (c) Alf Roberts.

9. Who played Buttons in the 1975 Street Christmas panto?

    (a) Len Fairclough. (b) Jerry Booth. (c) Ray Langton.

10. Who wrestled under the name of Stan the Terrible in 1964?

    (a) Stan Stennett. (b) Stan Ogden. (c) Stanley Baxter.

Answers on p. 103

A barmaid's lot!

1. Who was the barmaid who became landlady of The Rover's?

   (a) Tina Fowler. (b) Sally Webster. (c) Bet Lynch.
   (d) Annie Walker.

2. Which barmaid is famous for her hotpot specials?

   (a) Betty Turpin. (b) Bet Gilroy. (c) Alma Sedgewick.
   (d) Phyllis Pearce.

3. Which barmaid charmed Harry Hewitt into matrimony in 1961?

   (a) Ena Sharples. (b) Concepta Riley. (c) Joan Walker.

4. Who ran off with her best friend's boyfriend in 1988?

   (a) Stella Rigby. (b) Gloria Todd. (c) Gail Tilsley.

5. Which barmaid did Fred Gee marry in 1981?

   (a) Maggie Clegg. (b) Gloria Todd. (c) Eunice Nuttall.

6. Which barmaid was a battered wife in 1988?

   (a) Sandra Stubbs. (b) Sandra Gough. (c) Suzie Birchall.

7. Who was the flighty red-haired barmaid who lodged with Elsie Tanner in 1978?

   (a) Irma Barlow. (b) Suzie Birchall. (d) Ivy Tilsley.
   (d) Bet Lynch.

8. Whom did Jack Duckworth make a bee-line for in 1989?

   (a) Betty Turpin. (b) Tina Fowler. (c) Deirdre Barlow.

9. Which Welsh barmaid took over as housekeeper at The Rover's in 1989?

   (a) Megan Morgan. (b) Megan Edwards.
   (c) Vera Duckworth. (d) Dilys Laye.

10. Who used to run her own Cheshire pub in real life?

    (a) Salley Seddon. (b) Connie Clayton. (c) Betty Turpin.
    (d) Sarah Ridley.

Answers on p. 103

Cross The Road

1. Who did Mike Baldwin sell the factory to in August 1989?
2. Who developed the factory site into shops and houses?
3. Who organised an all-girl picket to get their redundancy money from Mike Baldwin?
4. Who were the first people to move into the new houses?
5. Who lives above the Kabin?
6. Emily had a shop for a while. What sort of shop was it?
7. Who lives at No. 4?
8. What is the name of the hairdresser's?
9. Who runs the hairdresser's?
10. Name her assistant.

Answers on p. 105

Animal Magic!

1. Who came home with a greyhound stray in 1989?
   (a) Jack Duckworth. (b) Don Brennan. (c) Sean Wilson.

2. Which cast regular owns racehorses in real life?
   (a) Mark Eden. (b) Roy Barraclough. (c) Bill Tarmey.
   (d) Bill Waddington.

3. Who got a job as a kennelmaid in Sheffield in 1982?
   (a) Lucille Hewitt. (b) Jenny Bradley.
   (c) Sharon Gaskell. (d) Mavis Riley.

4. Which famous Street animal star was recast in 1989?
   (a) Mavis Wilton's budgie.
   (b) The cat on the roof in the opening titles.
   (c) The cow at the back of Alf Roberts' Corner Shop.

5. Who kept a greyhound, secretly, in Annie Walker's cellar?
   (a) Fred Gee. (b) Eddie Yeats. (c) Stan Ogden.

6. Who owned a donkey called Dolores in 1972?
   (a) Alf Roberts. (b) Tommy Deakin. (c) Dave Smith.

7. Which pensioner had a cat called Bobbie?
   (a) Albert Tatlock. (b) Phyllis Pearce.
   (c) Minnie Caldwell.

8. How did the girls stop Mike Baldwin from getting rid of the factory cat?
   (a) Took it home. (b) Made it a member of their union.
   (c) Hid it. (d) Silenced its purr.

9. What happened to Eddie Yeats' guard dog?
   (a) It was stolen by thieves. (b) It went berserk.
   (c) It died.

10. Who adopted a pigeon called Gilbert which was eaten by Minnie Caldwell's cat?
    (a) Len Fairclough. (b) Alf Roberts. (c) Dennis Tanner.
    (d) Albert Tatlock.

Answers on p. 103

Sons and Daughters

1. What was Stan and Hilda Ogden's obnoxious son called?
   (a) Derek. (b) Dennis. (c) Trevor. (d) Julian.

2. Who is the daughter of runaway con-man Alan Bradley?
   (a) Jenny. (b) Julia. (c) Jean. (d) Sally.

3. What is the name of Jack and Vera Duckworth's tear-away offspring?
   (a) Nigel. (b) Ted. (c) Terry. (d) Thomas.

4. What is the name of Gail Tilsley's blonde-haired son?
   (a) Norman. (b) Nicky. (c) Neville. (d) Ned.

5. Who fostered two black children, Vernon and Lucy Foyle, in 1974?
   (a) The Duckworths. (b) The Bishops. (c) The Ogdens.
   (d) The Barlows.

6. Whose son was murdered outside a nightclub in 1989?
   (a) Vera Duckworth's. (b) Audrey Roberts'.
   (c) Ivy Brennan's. (d) Betty Turpin's.

7. Which 11-year-old ran away from an orphanage to be near his or her father in 1961?
   (a) Lucille Hewitt. (b) Eddie Yeats. (c) Dennis Tanner.
   (d) Jed Stone.

8. What was the name of Ken Barlow's daughter who married Mike Baldwin in 1986?
   (a) Sarah. (b) Sally. (c) Suzanne. (d) Susan.

9. Whose mother married Alf Roberts in 1985?
   (a) Billy Walker's. (b) Jenny Bradley's. (c) Gail Tilsley's.
   (d) Sally Seddon's.

10. Who gave birth to twins in 1965?
    (a) Elsie Tanner. (b) Valerie Barlow. (c) Emily Nugent.
    (d) Concepta Riley.

Answers on p. 103

Occupations

1. Which job did Eddie Yeats take over from Stan Ogden?
   (a) A milk round. (b) A window-cleaning business.
   (c) A pet shop. (d) A pie sales round.

2. What was Alf Roberts' job before he ran the Corner Shop?
   (a) Plumber. (b) Gas fitter. (c) GPO supervisor.

3. When Billy Walker left the army in the first month of the programme, what was his first job?
   (a) Policeman. (b) Decorator. (c) Car mechanic.

4. What kind of business did the Bonarti family open up in 1961?
   (a) Italian restaurant. (b) Ice cream business.
   (c) Tight-rope walking. (d) Delicatessen.

5. What did Elsie Tanner's fancy man Dave Smith run?
   (a) Laundry. (b) Betting shop. (c) Supermarket.

6. Who moved into The Rover's as a pot-man after his wife had died in a warehouse fire?
   (a) Fred Gee. (b) Len Fairclough. (c) Mike Baldwin.

7. What was Irishman Tommy Deakin's job in 1970?
   (a) Dustbinman. (b) Gardener. (c) Rag-and-bone man.

8. Who was Ken Barlow's first assistant when he went to edit then *Weatherfield Recorder*?
   (a) Suzie Birchall. (b) Gail Tilsley. (c) Sally Waterman.
   (d) Sarah Ridley.

9. What products did Derek Wilton end up selling in 1989 after he got the sack?
   (a) Biscuits. (b) Double-glazing. (c) Household brushes.
   (d) Balloons and novelties.

10. Who owned the Corner Shop when the series opened in December 1960?
    (a) Florrie Lindley. (b) Elsie Lappin. (c) Ida Barlow.
    (d) Ena Sharples.

Answers on p. 104

Funny Girls!

1. Who used to go 'tra-la-la' as she cleaned The Rover's?
   (a) Hilda Ogden. (b) Ivy Tilsley. (c) Annie Walker.

2. Who wears a curly blonde wig, has a voice like a corncrake, and works in the clothing factory?
   (a) Ida Clough. (b) Minnie Caldwell.
   (c) Vera Duckworth. (d) Sally Seddon.

3. In 1988, who went 'berserk' with her hubby's credit cards?
   (a) Audrey Roberts. (b) Gail Tilsley. (c) Susan Barlow.

4. Which Street star once played glamour roles in the 'Carry on . . .' films, including 'Carry on Cleo'?
   (a) Sue Nicholls. (b) Amanda Barrie. (c) Betty Driver.
   (d) Jean Alexander.

5. Who used the CB radio 'handle' Stardust Lil in 1983?
   (a) Bet Lynch. (b) Marion Willis. (c) Emily Bishop.

6. Which actress began as a stand-up club comedienne?
   (a) Jill Summers. (b) Lynne Perrie. (c) Violet Carson.
   (d) Pat Phoenix.

7. Who played an 'unamused' Queen Victoria in the Street's 'Britain through the Ages' tableau in 1977?
   (a) Ena Sharples. (b) Annie Walker. (c) Betty Turpin.
   (d) Mavis Riley.

8. Who had flying ducks and a 'muriel' painted on the wall of her living room?
   (a) Rene Bradshaw. (b) Blanche Hunt. (c) Hilda Ogden.
   (d) Martha Longhurst.

9. Who told the Street girls to withdraw all sexual favours – Lysistrata style – in 1970 over a football bus protest?
   (a) Ena Sharples. (b) Betty Turpin. (c) Elsie Tanner.
   (d) Annie Walker.

10. Who had a blonde 'hair-do' and a tattoo in 1964?
    (a) Irma Ogden. (b) Lucille Hewitt. (c) Sheila Birtles.

Answers on p. 104

Men in Uniform

1. Who wore a T-shirt that said 'I've made gravy under shellfire'?

   (a) Albert Tatlock. (b) Percy Sugden.
   (c) Len Fairclough.

2. Which actor was a Camel Corps commander in real life?

   (a) William Roache. (b) Johnny Briggs. (c) Nigel Pivaro.

3. Who joined the Parachute Regiment but failed the course?

   (a) Jack Duckworth. (b) Terry Duckworth.
   (c) Stan Ogden. (d) Len Fairclough.

4. Who served on Russian convoys with the Royal Navy?

   (a) Leonard Swindley. (b) Charlie Moffitt.
   (c) Len Fairclough. (d) Jack Walker.

5. Who was Elsie Tanner's Chief Petty Officer boyfriend?

   (a) Fred Gee. (b) Frank Pemberton. (c) Steve Tanner.
   (d) Bill Gregory.

6. Which old soldier refused to ride in Ken Barlow's Beetle because it was 'a Jerry car'?

   (a) Percy Sugden. (b) Jack Walker. (c) Albert Tatlock.

7. What was Dot Greenhalgh's American soldier boyfriend called in 1968?

   (a) Greg Dyke. (b) Gregg Flint. (c) Greg Gregory.

8. Who represented the Lancashire Fusiliers at Albert Tatlock's 80th birthday party in 1975?

   (a) A drummer. (b) A sergeant major. (c) A bugler.
   (d) The Colonel in Chief.

9. Whose first husband Arnold was in the merchant navy?

   (a) Elsie Tanner's. (b) Rita Fairclough's.
   (c) Mavis Riley's.

10. Who left the Street cast to become Captain Mainwaring in *Dad's Army*?

    (a) Peter Adamson. (b) Nigel Pivaro. (c) Arthur Lowe.

Answers on p. 104

Neighbours

1. Which family lives next door to The Rover's Return?
   (a) The Ogdens. (b) The Websters. (c) The Barlows.
   (d) The Duckworths.

2. Who lives at Number 9 Coronation Street?
   (a) Mike Baldwin. (b) The Duckworths. (c) Gail Tilsley.

3. Who is Rita's Fairclough's lodger above The Kabin?
   (a) Curly Watts. (b) Mavis Wilton. (c) Tina Fowler.

4. Which house did the Ogdens buy for £575 in 1964?
   (a) The Corner Shop. (b) Number 13. (c) Number 7.
   (d) The Community Centre flat.

5. Who lived at Number 13 Coronation Street – next door to
   the Tanners – between 1960 and 1962?
   (a) May and Christine Hardman. (b) Albert Tatlock.
   (c) Minnie Caldwell. (d) Ena Sharples.

6. Which Street landmark was demolished in 1968?
   (a) The Rover's Return. (b) The Corner Shop.
   (c) The Glad Tidings Mission. (d) Alf's Mini Market.

7. Where did Stan Ogden's fancy woman live?
   (a) Sebastapol Terrace. (b) Inkerman Street.
   (c) Coronation Place. (d) Rosamund Street.

8. What were the Welsh family called who moved into the
   Corner Shop in 1975?
   (a) Jones. (b) Hopkins. (c) Griffiths. (d) Morris.

9. Which house collapsed, and was demolished and rebuilt
   by Len Fairclough?
   (a) Number 7. (b) Number 11. (c) Number 15.

10. Who lives in a luxury flat?
    (a) Terry Duckworth. (b) Billy Walker.
    (c) Mike Baldwin.

Answers on p. 104

Weddings of The Nineties

1. Who provided the flowers for Mike Baldwin and Jackie Ingram's wedding?

2. What was the address where Mike Baldwin and Jackie made their home after the wedding?

3. As the wedding of Mike and Jackie approached, how much was their company owed in bad debt?

4. On what date did Alma and Mike marry?

5. Which of Mike's old girlfriends attended the wedding?

6. What unusual thing happened during Terry and Lisa Duckworth's wedding?

7. Who was Terry's Best Man?

8. How did Bet and Charlie arrive at Reg and Maureen's wedding?

9. Ted Sullivan had just retired when he married Rita. What had his job been?

10. Who refused to attend Ted and Rita's wedding?

Answers on p. 105

SECTION TWO:
Coronation Street

ADDICTS

Happy Families

1. Albert Tatlock was 'Uncle Albert' to Ken Barlow, but whose real uncle was he?

2. Name Len Fairclough's son?

3. Who attempted suicide after her soldier son was killed in Northern Ireland in 1975?

4. Which Street son was ashamed of his parents?

5. Name Sally Webster's sister?

6. Name Hilda Ogden's grandchildren from her son Trevor?

7. What was the name of Vera Duckworth's mother?

8. What was Audrey Roberts' maiden name?

9. Who was the surprise guest at Susan and Mike Baldwin's wedding?

10. What was Ken Barlow's dad called?

11. For whom did Len Fairclough's first wife leave him in 1962?

12. What was the name of Sandra Stubbs' son?

13. Whose mum was born as middle class Beaumont of Clitheroe?

14. Whose daughter emigrated to Canada in December 1961?

15. Who was thought to be baby Sarah Louise Tilsley's father after Gail's affair in 1986?

Answers on p. 106

Wedding Bells

1. Who was Don Brennan's best man when he married Ivy?

2. Who was Bet Lynch's bridesmaid?

3. Which couple got cold feet about marriage in 1984?

4. What were Audrey Roberts' old school friends called who turned up at her wedding to Alf?

5. Why did Eddie Yeats and Marion Willis finally marry?

6. Who were Deirdre's bridesmaids when she married Ken Barlow in 1981?

7. Who did Fred Gee marry to get his own pub?

8. Which Street bride was said by her husband to have 'the best pair of pins since Betty Grable'?

9. What was the maiden name of Ken Barlow's first wife in 1961?

10. Who was the betting shop owner that Rita jilted in 1975 to marry Len Fairclough?

11. Which Street actors married in real life in 1972?

12. Why were Elsie Tanner's wedding celebrations blighted in 1967?

13. Who married for the third time in 1981?

14. Which Street ditherer finally tied the knot in 1988?

15. Who gave Joan Walker away in March 1961, at the Street's first wedding?

Answers on p. 106

Women Of The Nineties

1. When Rovers barmaid Tina Fowler went on her first date with builder Eddie Ramsden where did they go?

2. What did Ivy Brennan become obsessed with attending in 1990?

3. What is Liz McDonald's nickname for her husband Jim?

4. Name the plumber Deirdre Barlow had an affair with.

5. After Kimberley Taylor left Curly for the first time, who did she fall in love with?

6. Where did Emily Bishop plan to move to in 1991?

7. What was Jackie Ingram's middle name?

8. Alma and Gail set up a company to run the café. What was it called?

9. What was Wendy Crozier's address?

10. Which Street woman did Alf ask to be Mayoress when Audrey went off the idea?

Answers on p. 116

Men Of The Nineties

1. Phil Jennings, Deirdre Barlow's flash boyfriend, had a flash car. What was its registration number?

2. When is Ken Barlow's birthday?

3. What is Mike Baldwin's middle name?

4. Where does Alec Gilroy work and live?

5. Name the photographer who took a shine to Raquel.

6. Name Mayor Alf Roberts' driver.

7. Which Street man became known as 'The Bird Man of Weatherfield' in 1994?

8. Which Street man is left-handed?

9. What is Des Barnes' profession?

10. Which footballer did Martin Platt accidentally injure?

Answers on p. 116

Drink to Me Only . . .

1. What were Hilda Ogden's two favourite tipples?

2. Who were the two Street men had up for drunken driving?

3. Who developed a drink problem in 1973 and came to blows with Elsie Howard?

4. Which favourite drink did Albert Tatlock like to cadge in the Rover's?

5. What is the name of the pub that mainly rivals The Rover's Return in Weatherfield?

6. What was the name of The Rover's relief barmaid engaged by Fred Gee when he took over in April 1984?

7. Who was temporary landlord of the Rover's prior to Bet Lynch taking over in 1985?

8. Who fell down the cellar steps of the Rover's in 1982 and threatened to sue Annie Walker?

9. Who was the tough relief manager who suspended Fred Gee for drinking free Scotch?

10. Why did The Rover's have to close down in March 1979?

11. Which barmaid was wrongly accused of stealing £5 in 1977?

12. Who drank too much beer at a home-brewing session in 1965?

13. Who enjoyed a tearful farewell 'do' at The Rover's before emigrating in 1961?

14. Which pub was Fred Gee offered first by the brewery in 1978?

15. What was the stage name of the exotic-dancer/barmaid who brought new life to The Rover's in 1989?

Answers on p. 106

Answer the following questions about the blonde in our picture:

1. Who is she?

2. Why is she wearing a crash helmet?

3. What injury did she sustain?

4. What is the name of her husband in the programme?

5. What is the name of her mischievous sister?

6. Where does she work?

7. What was her maiden name?

8. Who did she lodge with before she got married?

9. Which number house does she live at now?

10. In what year did she join the series?

Answers on p. 106

Family Fortunes (1): The Ogdens

1. What was Hilda's maiden name?

2. What mystic 'gift' did she think she had?

3. Which lodger did she enjoy washing and ironing for after Stan's death?

4. What was Stan's job before 1964?

5. Next to ale, what – or who – was Stan's vice?

6. What did Stan and Hilda buy for their daughter Irma in 1965?

7. Who was Stan's great 'business' mate in the 1970s?

8. How did Hilda acquire her famous flying ducks?

9. Who paid for Hilda's farewell 'do' when she left the Street in 1987?

10. Who did she go to keep house for?

11. What fate befell her when she went to prepare her new employer's retirement home?

12. Which pensioner became Hilda's persistent suitor?

13. What title did the Newton Abbott Stan Odgen Appreciation Society bestow on its hero?

14. What physical complaint did Stan suffer with for years?

15. Who were the actors who played Stan and Hilda Ogden?

Answers on p. 107

Family Favourites

1. Which two families went to war over goods on 'tick' in 1974?

2. Which family head took umbrage over his daughter's choice of husband in 1986?

3. Which family did a moonlit flit from the Street in 1975?

4. Which close family suffered a sudden and horrific bereavement in early 1989?

5. Which two families fell out over an unpaid taxi fare in August 1988?

6. Which family couple threatened to go their separate ways over a domestic quarrel in June 1989?

7. Which family pair fell out over a car driving dispute in September 1989?

8. Which two unlikely families were united in marriage in December 1965?

9. Which family lost a dearly loved dad in 1970?

10. Which family moved into the Street in January 1985?

11. Which family emigrated to Canada in 1961?

12. Which family left the Street briefly, and then moved back into Number 5 in the 1980s?

13. Which ice cream selling family fell foul of Hilda Ogden in June 1966?

14. Which family got in trouble with the Inland Revenue in 1989?

15. Which is the longest surviving family in the Street?

Answers on p. 107

The Young Ones

1. In 1988, which Street teenage girl was keen on Martin Platt?

2. Who did Shirley Armitage share a flat with in 1988?

3. Which young Street regular plays guitar in a Country and Western music group in real life?

4. Which Street tear-away ran off with Peter Jackson's wife Linda?

5. Which 17-year-old came between husband and wife in 1988?

6. Which young couple made a bid for ownership of the garage after Brian Tilsley died?

7. Who gave her life savings to her daughter Vera in 1966?

8. Which young husband had an affair with flirtatious Glenda Fox in 1981?

9. Who gave a foster home to John Spencer in 1981?

10. Which young girl fell for Gordon Clegg in 1968?

11. Whose mad-cap son fell for shop girl Sandra Petty in 1965?

12. Which young lodger was pitched out of her digs by landlady Elsie Tanner in 1979?

13. Who fell for uppercrust Michelle Robinson in 1985 but failed to scale the class barrier?

14. Which sixth form schoolgirl became pregnant in 1985?

15. Which young blonde joined The Rover's bar staff in 1989?

Answers on p. 107

Action Replay (2)

1. Who is the actress in the bridal gown?
2. Which dithery spinster did she play in 1964?
3. What happened when she got wedding day wobbles?
4. What was unusual about the marriage proposal?
5. Who was the bride-groom-to-be?
6. How many times has she married since?
7. With whom did she go to the altar last?
8. Where did she work throughout the eighties?
9. Who is the other character in the photograph?
10. And what event took her out of the series?

Answers on p. 107

Bettabuys

1. Name the member of the Bettabuys staff Reg Holdsworth was having an affair with in 1990.

2. Who won the 1991 Bettabuys trolley race?

3. Who was the designer of the Bettabuys 1991 carnival float?

4. Who is head of the Bettabuys Empire?

5. Name the graduate trainee who turned out to be the boss's daughter.

6. Which Street resident was caught shop-lifting from Bettabuys?

7. Who became a trainee manager at Bettabuys in 1993?

8. When Brendan Scott was area manager for Bettabuys, Weatherfield, what was the name of his secretary?

9. Who became manager of Bettabuys, Weatherfield in 1993?

10. Who was re-employed at Bettabuys in 1994?

Answers on p. 116

Laughter Makers

1. Who is the comic nosey parker in the cloth cap?

2. Which actor was a wartime music hall comic called 'Witty Willie'?

3. Who secretly learned to play 'Beautiful Dreamer' on the piano in the Rover's after being banned from the keyboard by Annie Walker?

4. Who was the gap-toothed Scouse actor who played Eddie Yeats?

5. Who called her husband 'chuck'?

6. Who went to a computer dating agency and was paired with his wife?

7. Who sang 'We're A Couple of Swells' in a talent contest in 1984?

8. Who did a Hilda Baker impression at the 1969 Christmas party?

9. Who were the two fatties dressed as babies in a sponsored pram race in 1978?

10. Once she was Vera Hopkins in the Street. What comic character does Kathy Staff play in *Last of the Summer Wine*?

11. Whose great shame was that she once played Lady Godiva in a body stocking?

12. Which great Street actor left to do a sitcom called *Pardon the Expression*?

13. Whose 'male' budgie laid an egg?

14. Who was accused of watering The Rover's gin in 1971?

15. Who rescued the wrong cat from the railway viaduct in 1968?

Answers on p. 108

Family Fortunes (2): The Barlows

1. How many sons did Frank Barlow have?

2. What was Frank's wife called?

3. Which son despised Frank's lack of education?

4. What was the name of the footballing son?

5. How long has Ken Barlow been in the series?

6. Name the actor who plays Ken?

7. How many times has Ken been married?

8. Which wife presented him with twins?

9. Who romantically ensnared his wife in 1983?

10. What was Ken's married daughter called?

11. Who was Frank Barlow's old Post Office chum?

12. What is the name of Deirdre Barlow's daughter?

13. What was Ken Barlow's original profession?

14. Who did Ken controversially appoint as community play leader in 1976?

15. Who slipped away to a secret Register Office wedding with David Barlow in 1965?

Answers on p. 108

Guys and Dolls

1. Which guy used to clean windows for a living and had a 'glass' back?

2. Which 'dolly' beautician did Ken Barlow take to Mike Baldwin's flat-warming party in 1981?

3. Who swept Elsie Tanner off to a new life in Portugal?

4. Who was the redhead who fascinated both Alf Roberts and Len Fairclough?

5. What was the name of Chalkie Whiteley's grandson who accompanied him to Australia?

6. Which merry widow led Martin Platt a dance in 1988?

7. Who was the Street rotter who deserted his wife and child in 1980?

8. Which bottle blonde became Mike Baldwin's live-in mistress in 1977?

9. Who was the ageing Street man who nearly married the young Christine Hardman in the 1960s?

10. Which doe-eyed devotee fell for the Superintendent of the Glad Tidings Mission in 1964?

11. Whose ex-wife Laura bailed him out of a £2,000 debt in 1972?

12. Which fiery redhead took up with a young art teacher in 1964?

13. Which old soldier has a permanent soft spot for Emily Bishop?

14. Which schoolgirl fell under the spell of Terry Duckworth in 1985?

15. Who was Mavis Riley's camping and hiking boyfriend in 1983?

Answers on p. 108

Action Replay (3)

1. Who is this actor?

2. Which character does he play?

3. Who is his TV wife?

4. Where is their temporary flat sited?

5. Why did he have less occasion to feel cheery in 1989?

6. Who selected a wife for him in 1978?

7. Who was his great rival in love?

8. What is the actor's unusual hobby?

9. Who did he take on a summer cruise in 1982 instead of his girlfriend?

10. What did he buy his girlfriend on a weekend in Kendal in 1976?

Answers on p. 108

Find the Surnames

We'll give you the christian names of these famous Street characters and actors. You supply the surname:

1. A barmaid called Elizabeth Theresa.

2. A fatman called George Edward.

3. A shopkeeper called Alfred Sydney.

4. A rogue called Raymond Anthony.

5. A brawler called Leonard Frankland.

6. A housewife called Deirdre Anne.

7. A teenage actress called Sally Ann.

8. A baby called Sarah Louise.

9. A comic actor called William Cleworth.

10. A buxom barmaid often addressed by Annie Walker as Elizabeth.

11. A famous writer whose real name is Anthony McVay Simpson.

12. A toothy, plump lady called Marion.

13. Her name was Elsie and she came before Elsie Tanner.

14. His name was Walter and he cleaned windows in 1963.

15. A shocking snob who much preferred her Sunday name – Anne.

Answers on p. 109

Senior Citizens

1. Who did Ena Sharples do verbal battle with in Episode One?

2. What was her famous visual trade mark?

3. Which OAP took a fancy to Percy Sugden?

4. Who was Percy's rival in love?

5. Which current OAP is a master cook?

6. Which OAP lived at No 5 in 1962.

7. Who did she take in as a lodger?

8. Who was the female super-snoop in 1961?

9. Which OAP flew to Nebraska in 1965?

10. Which OAP was knocked unconscious in a betting shop raid?

11. What was Sally Webster's uncle called?

12. Which old variety comic played the role?

13. Which OAP carried a miniature dog around in a holdall?

14. Which famous radio actor played the role?

15. Which veteran Street actor died in 1984 aged 88?

Answers on p. 109

The Corner Shop In The Nineties

1. On what date did Reg Holsworth take over the Corner Shop?

2. What time does Reg open the shop?

3. What did Reg plan to do with the Corner Shop on Sundays?

4. How long did Brendan Scott run the Corner Shop for?

5. Name Brendan Scott's wife.

6. Who had a heart attack in the shop?

7. Which two Street ladies helped Brendan Scott during his time at the shop?

8. Who bought the shop from Debi Scott?

9. Who lives in the flat above the Corner Shop?

10. What illegal product did Reg sell in the shop?

Answers on p. 117

Family Fortunes (3): The Tilsleys

1. What were the names of Brian's parents?

2. What early job did Brian do in 1981?

3. Why was he arrested for unlawful wounding?

4. In which year did Brian and Gail marry?

5. What was her maiden name?

6. When toddler Nicky disappeared in 1982, where was he found?

7. When Brian worked in the Gulf, what was the name of Gail's admirer?

8. In what did Brian invest his £2,000 savings from Qatar?

9. What grave news reached Ivy Tilsley in 1984?

10. Which actress portrays Ivy?

11. When she re-married in 1988, what was Ivy's new surname?

12. What was the name of Ivy's boyfriend who made a pass at Gail in 1984?

13. What did Brian do as a consequence?

14. What were Bert Tilsley's two hobbies?

15. What was the name of Gail's Welsh friend in 1974?

Answers on p. 109

1. What is the name of the actress?

2. What character does she play?

3. Why was she in mourning in 1989?

4. What is the name of the boy in the picture?

5. What is the name of his sister?

6. Who is the character's father-in-law?

7. What is the name of the Australian with whom she had an affair?

8. Which 'toy boy' entered her life in 1989?

9. What business did her late husband run?

10. What did she learn about her own parentage?

Answers on p. 109

Trade Marks

Identify the characters by the following 'trade marks':

1. Trilby hat and white overall.

2. Three hair curlers and a turban.

3. Gap-toothed grin and woolly bob hat.

4. Open necked check shirt and beer belly.

5. Old flat 'at with a tear in one side.

6. Hairnet and iron jaw.

7. Outrageous earrings including parakeets on hoops.

8. Silver hair with blue rinse.

9. Foghorn voice and bubbly blonde hair-do.

10. Beefcake body under green overalls.

11. Flaming red hair and plunging busty neckline.

12. Sharp suit and small cigar.

13. Blonde hair and owlish spectacles.

14. Pint-size blonde with wicked tongue.

15. Street ditherer whose catch-phrase is 'Well, I don't really know!'

Answers on p. 110

Jumbled Names

Rearrange the letters to make the names of well-known characters:

1. Nek Larbow
2. Nel Roifghaulc
3. Ane Plesrhas
4. Kiem Dwinlab
5. Deied Teyas
6. Selie Natern
7. Blaert Lkoctat
8. Lagi Leystil
9. Rave Wrthokcud
10. Edj Etson
11. Nleorda Leydwins
12. Thraam Thursgnol
13. Teb Yilgor
14. Zieus Lchaiblr
15. Niean Kwerla

Answers on p. 110

Coronation Street Egg Heads

1. Who was the Street university 'egg head' who was jailed for taking part in an anti-Vietnam war demonstration in 1967?

2. Who is the ex-refuse collector with 8 'O' Levels and 2 'A' levels to his name?

3. Who was the pretty Street teenager hoping to go off to university in 1989?

4. Who became a Fellow of the Institute of British Photography?

5. Who became an accountant and took a job in London in 1969?

6. Who regarded herself as an intellectual, able to converse as an equal with Ken Barlow?

7. Who wrote a wedding speech with quotations from Shaw, then was not selected for best man?

8. Who had an affair with a 33-year-old university librarian when he was 21?

9. Who left the Street to become a Civil Service statistician in 1964?

10. Who took up with School of Design art teacher David Graham?

11. Who was the headmaster of Bessie Street School in 1972?

12. Which character, with literary leanings, wrote a novel in 1976?

13. Who joined a literary class and met Victor Pendlebury in 1982?

14. Which Street actor speaks fluent Arabic and why?

15. Who failed The Rover's by one point in a Brainiest Pub Contest in 1985?

Answers on p. 110

1. Who is the actor in the picture?
2. Who did he play?
3. Who is the woman next to him?
4. Why is she in tears?
5. Which army regiment did this old soldier serve in?
6. What was the name of his niece who died?
7. What is the name of his fractious grown-up daughter?
8. What number Coronation Street did he live at?
9. Who was the widow who proposed to him in 1965?
10. What job did he perform in his retirement?

Answers on p. 110

Family Fortunes (4): The Tanners

1. Who first whisked Elsie Tanner to the altar?

2. How many children did she have?

3. Who was the actress who played Elsie?

4. Where does Elsie live now?

5. What was her wastrel son called?

6. What was his first job attempt?

7. When he became a rock singer what name did he use?

8. For what offence was he committed to Wormwood Scrubs?

9. What was Dennis's elder sister called?

10. Who was the new Tanner on the scene in 1967?

11. What nationality was he?

12. What was his occupation?

13. What fate befell him?

14. When did Pat Phoenix die?

15. Who did she marry in real life that year?

Answers on p. 111

Nick Names

1. Who was affectionately known as 'Big Oggie'?

2. Which actor was known by friends as 'Bunny'?

3. What is Curly Watts proper Christian name?

4. What was Sonny Jim's proper name?

5. Who had a mate called Monkey Gibbon?

6. What was Walter Potts' singing name?

7. Which character is sometimes called 'Duck Egg'?

8. What was Mr Whiteley, the dustbinman known as?

9. Whose CB radio 'handle' was Slim Jim?

10. Who is also known as 'Jack the Lad'?

11. Who did Fleet Street dub 'The Tart with a Heart'?

12. What did SODU stand for?

13. Who was 'Tickler' Murphy?

14. Who had a greyhound called 'Little Titch'?

15. What was snake dancer Eunice Bond's stage name?

Answers on p. 111

Reg, Maureen And Maud Too . . .

1. What are Maud Grimes' favourite flowers?

2. Where was Reg planning on taking Maureen for the honeymoon which never quite came off?

3. On Maureen's wedding day what did Maud give her?

4. Where do Maud's other daughter, Peggy, and her husband, Clive, live?

5. When Reg lived on his own what sensual item of bedroom furniture did he have in his flat?

6. What is Maureen's middle name?

7. Who agreed to look after Maud while Reg and Maureen were on honeymoon?

8. What kind of tea does Reg drink?

9. What was the date of Reg and Maureen's wedding?

10. Name the church where the wedding took place and the place where the reception was held.

Answers on p. 117

Forgotten Stars

Which roles did the following celebrities and TV personalities play in Coronation Street?

1. Maudie Edwards.

2. Arthur Lowe.

3. Doris Hare.

4. *Emmerdale Farm*'s Seth Armstrong (Stan Richards).

5. *EastEnders*' Pete Beale (Peter Dean).

6. Reginald Marsh.

7. Jack Smethurst.

8. The Duke of Bedford.

9. William Moore.

10. Stan Stennett.

11. Amanda Barrie.

12. Angela Pleasance.

13. Leonard Sachs.

14. Petty Officer Jack Watson.

15. Patrick Troughton.

Answers on p. 111

1. Who is this actress?

2. What character does she play?

3. What civic role did she play in 1989?

4. As a bored housewife, who did she get romantically involved with?

5. What was her first husband called?

6. What is her present husband's occupation?

7. What is her daughter's name?

8. Who did she work for when she first arrived in the Street?

9. Why did she panic when a lorry crashed into the Rover's?

10. What does she wear on screen that she doesn't in real life?

Answers on p. 111

Trouble Makers

1. Who undermined Ken and Deirdre's marriage in 1983?

2. Who terrorised Emily Bishop in 1981?

3. Which Street 'con man' tried to part Rita Fairclough from her cash?

4. Who got Jerry Booth into debt in 1964?

5. Who forced Sheila Birtles to near suicide?

6. Who tried to use non-union labour in his factory?

7. Who battererd Sandra Stubbs in 1988?

8. Who seduced Brian Tilsley's wife in 1986?

9. Who ran off with Pete Jackson's wife in 1988?

10. Whose best mate put him under suspicion for theft in 1979?

11. Who forced Bet Lynch into deep depression in 1979?

12. Who had her clothes slashed to bits for stealing someone else's husband in 1981?

13. Who maliciously cited Ken Barlow in a divorce in 1979?

14. Who got Annie Walker in hot water for drinking after hours?

15. Whose boyfriend developed worrying Jekyll and Hyde tendencies in 1980?

Answers on p. 112

Sick Parade

1. Who collapsed on the floor of the Glad Tidings Mission in 1961?

2. Who collapsed behind the wheel of a Jaguar in 1965?

3. Whose leg injury ended his soccer career?

4. Who was struck down by a brain tumour in 1967?

5. Who broke his arm for the second time in 1969?

6. Who ended up in hospital on a lorry run to Newcastle?

7. Why did Elsie Tanner end up in hospital in 1973?

8. Who gave Mike Baldwin's new girlfriend a black eye in 1977?

9. Which OAP went down with severe food poisoning in 1978?

10. Who was crestfallen to find he was allergic to beer?

11. Who suffered a mental breakdown in 1983?

12. Who collapsed under the strain of nursing her husband in 1984?

13. Who was paralysed after a coach crash in 1969?

14. Why was Mike Baldwin furious with his pregnant wife Susan?

15. What was the name of the sick relative who Audrey Roberts visited in Canada in 1988?

Answers on p. 112

Family Favourites (5): The Faircloughs

1. What happened to Len Fairclough's parents?

2. Where did he spend his war years?

3. What was his Civvy Street trade?

4. When he became self-employed where did he site his yard?

5. Who did Len propose to – several times – after his first wife divorced him?

6. Whose second wife was he once engaged to?

7. Why was Len late for his wedding to Rita Littlewood?

8. How did Rita spend her teenage years?

9. Where did she meet Councillor Len Fairclough?

10. Why did she break off her engagement in 1977?

11. Which teenage girl did Rita first become a 'mother' to?

12. And who was the second teenager she took under her wing?

13. Who was the detective inspector who wanted her to spend Christmas with him after Len's death?

14. Who is Rita's best mate in The Kabin?

15. Who is the shopkeeper who has always been her best male pal?

Answers on p. 112

Action Replay (7)

1. What is the name of the actor?
2. Which character did he play?
3. Who did he live with?
4. What did he do behind her back?
5. Whose name did he fraudulently use?
6. What business did he set up?
7. What was the name of his male assistant?
8. Which young female did he sexually harrass?
9. What is the name of his daughter?
10. Which Street actress is the actor married to in real life?

Answers on p. 112

Cars of the Stars

1. Which husband and wife team took up banger racing in 1989?

2. What type of vehicle did Harry Hewitt drive?

3. What fancy saloon does Mike Baldwin drive?

4. What type of car did Annie Walker purchase?

5. What does Don Brennan drive to work?

6. What type of vehicle was Stan Ogden most familiar with?

7. Which duties did Terry Duckworth perform for Mike Baldwin in 1988?

8. Which spinster passed her driving test in 1965?

9. Why did the coach crash on the Street trip to Windermere in 1969?

10. Who opened a garage in Canal Street in 1970?

11. Who did he take into partnership?

12. Who was flung through a car windscreen in 1980?

13. Which Street 'fattie' rode a dustcart in 1981?

14. Which van driver had an eye for Ivy Tilsley in 1985?

15. Which ex-schoolteacher tried taxi driving in 1975?

Answers on p. 113

Blonde Bombshells

1. Which warring factory blondes are good friends in private?

2. Which blonde landlady was a Street tartar?

3. Which blonde 'Mr Muscles' ran a garage?

4. Which blonde barmaid had an illegitimate son?

5. Which curly-headed blonde was an ex-matelot?

6. Which dizzy blonde leads Alf Roberts a dance?

7. Which busty blonde teases Jack Duckworth?

8. Which blonde housewife became a local councillor?

9. Which ample blonde married Fred Gee?

10. Which dithery blonde hankered over Derek Wilton?

11. Which middle-aged blonde once owned the Corner Shop?

12. Which blonde hotel receptionist fell for Ken Barlow?

13. Which Street mum has a blonde-haired young son?

14. Who bought a blonde wig to cheer up her 'charlady' image?

15. What is the name of Alan Bradley's strawberry blonde daughter?

Answers on p. 113

Raquel

1. In early 1994 Raquel had her first real modelling job. What was it for?

2. What month was Raquel on the calendar?

3. Who was Raquel's partner during the calendar shoot?

4. Who escorted Raquel to Reg and Maureen's wedding?

5. At Reg and Maureen's wedding who chatted Raquel up?

6. Who was behind Raquel's fake modelling job?

7. Name the footballer Raquel went out with for a time.

8. Who gave Raquel French lessons?

9. Who did Raquel push into Weatherfield Dock?

10. What was the name of the modelling school Raquel went to, and in what part of London was it?

Answers on p. 117

The Fugitives

1. Who eloped to Gretna Green then had second thoughts?

2. Which family left the Street overnight in disgrace?

3. Who ran off with his best friend's wife?

4. Who was last seen heading for Birmingham with a travelling salesman?

5. Who left Weatherfield for Scarborough with her illegitimate baby?

6. Who left the Street for retirement in Whalley Bridge?

7. Who left Weatherfield to live in Zaire?

8. Who left Coronation Street in 1989 on the run from the police?

9. Who gave Billy Walker a farewell punch on the nose then left the Street in 1984?

10. Who went off to run Gregory's Bar in the Algarve?

11. Which Street fugitive lives in Castle Blaney, Eire?

12. Who went back to live in his hometown – Newcastle?

13. Which Street pair run a country club in Kenilworth?

14. Who left to start a new life in Holland in 1978?

15. Where did Florrie Lindley emigrate to to make a fresh start in 1965?

Answers on p. 113

1. What are the names of these two actors?

2. Which characters do they play?

3. What is the name of their 'awful' son?

4. Why did she cut up all her husband's trousers in 1989?

5. Who is her best mate?

6. Where did they work together?

7. Who is his boss?

8. Which number Coronation Street do they live at?

9. Whose daughter did their son make pregnant in 1985?

10. What market stall venture did Elsie Tanner join them in in 1981?

Answers on p. 113

Family Fortunes (6): The Websters

1. What was Kevin's dad called?

2. Name Kevin's sister?

3. What was their father's trade?

4. Where did the family finally move to?

5. Who refused to leave with them?

6. Which girl did he take up with?

7. Where did Kevin find employment?

8. What happened to his boss?

9. Where does his bubbly wife work?

10. Which house did the young couple buy?

11. Who was the previous owner?

12. Who was the cuckoo in the nest?

13. Which actor plays Kevin?

14. Who plays his pretty blonde wife?

15. Who did Kevin's father marry?

Answers on p. 114

Pot Pourri

1. Whose boat sank like a stone when it was launched?

2. Who lost his life to a gunman because he stood his ground?

3. Who warmed a budgie egg in her bra to see if it would hatch?

4. Who was barred by the Ogdens as a 'domino sharp'?

5. Who brought the factory from Mike Baldwin in 1989?

6. Who did he put in charge of gate security?

7. Who was involved in a toy sales war in 1989?

8. What was the name of the rival salesman?

9. Which new soap toppled *Coronation Street* from the ratings in 1985?

10. Who crashed Alf Roberts' treasured sports car?

11. After her home was demolished in Omdurman Street, who did Phyllis Pearce move in with?

12. Who nearly died in a fire at The Rover's in 1985?

13. Who accidentally caused the blaze?

14. Who tried to tempt widowed Hilda Ogden to a new life in his little bungalow?

15. Who was brought up in Gas Street, got pregnant at 16, and married a merchant sailor?

Answers on p. 114

Family Fortunes (7): The Walkers

1. What was Jack Walker's haughty wife called?

2. What was the name of their daughter?

3. Who did their son Billy propose marriage to, before she met Ken Barlow?

4. When Billy was suspected of fiddling in the pub, which island did he flee to?

5. When did Jack Walker die?

6. Which actor played the role?

7. Why were the scriptwriters forced to kill off Jack?

8. Where did Jack's daughter live?

9. Who was dubbed 'the first lady of Weatherfield'?

10. Which early job did she try to keep quiet about?

11. Which civic role came her way in 1973?

12. Who became her reluctant part-time chauffeur?

13. Which buxom barmaid was her Rover's confidante?

14. What year did she leave the Street?

15. Where did she go to live?

Answers on p. 114

1. Who is this actor?
2. Which character does he play?
3. What business does he run?
4. What is the name of his spendthrift wife?
5. What was the name of his first wife?
6. Whom did he marry in 1978?
7. Which industry did he retire from, aged 53?
8. Who did he court and really want to marry for ages?
9. Who defeated him in a local council election?
10. Which army unit did he serve in?

Answers on p. 114

Family Fortunes (8): The Claytons

1. How many Claytons moved into Coronation Street?

2. What were their christian names?

3. In which year did they move in?

4. Which number house did they buy?

5. Who did they buy it from?

6. What was the name of their noisy next door neighbours?

7. Who was the brainy member of the family?

8. What was the mother's occupation?

9. What did the happy-go-lucky dad do for fun?

10. Which actor played the father?

11. Who played mum?

12. Which daughter got into trouble with Terry Duckworth?

13. What was her decision when he proposed marriage?

14. Who was the famous past tenant of the house they lived in?

15. When did they leave the Street?

Answers on p. 115

Food for Thought

1. Whose standing order in Jim's Cafe was always 'a nice cup of tea and a toasted tea cake'?

2. What were Sheila Birtles and Doreen Lostock famous for?

3. Whose brother ran a local chip shop?

4. Who are the current owner's of Jim's Cafe?

5. Who got food poisoning from his own allotment?

6. Which roly poly grocer runs the Mini Market?

7. Who asked for 'half a dozen fancies, and no eclairs'?

8. Who turned out to be allergic to eggs in 1980?

9. Who did Florrie Lindley sell the Corner Shop to?

10. Who began an ice cream business in 1966?

11. Why did Alf Roberts lose his lunchtime sandwich trade in 1989?

12. Who had an accident with a lorry-load of bananas?

13. Which OAP claims to be a master cook?

14. Which OAP was made redundant from the cafe in 1989?

15. Who did Ken Barlow charm with his steak au poivre in July, 1979?

Answers on p. 115

Family Fortunes (9): The Duckworths

1. Which Duckworth tried to run a market stall?

2. Who is Vera's best mate?

3. Where did Terry work when he left the army?

4. What 'goodies' did he bring home to mum?

5. Which actor plays Jack?

6. Which actress plays Vera?

7. Which actor played Terry?

8. Who is Jack's current boss?

9. Who was Terry's late business partner?

10. What was sex-starved Jack's master plan in 1987?

11. Where was Vera made redundant from in 1989?

12. Who was her old boss?

13. In which year did Vera celebrate her 50th birthday?

14. How much did Vera win at bingo in 1984?

15. Which Duckworth won a seaside holiday in 1980?

Answers on p. 115

1. Who is this actress?

2. Which character does she play?

3. Where has she worked as both barmaid and landlady?

4. What was the name of her illegitimate, adopted son?

5. Whose mother thought she was 'common' and not good enough for her son?

6. In which year did she win her spurs as a landlady?

7. When she left the country, in debt, where was she found working?

8. Who did she decline to marry in June 1978?

9. Who led her on, then let her down in 1975?

10. Who was her first Street beau in 1970?

Answers on p. 115

Affairs Of The Nineties

1. Name the woman Ken Barlow had an affair with in the early 1990s.

2. Name the flash man whom Deirdre dated in 1990.

3. Who was Lisa Duckworth having an affair with before she died?

4. Name the man who took a shine to Sally Webster in 1993.

5. Who did Maureen Naylor have a one-night stand with?

6. Who tried to seduce Mavis Wilton in February 1990?

7. Name the woman Andy McDonald had his first affair with.

8. Name the man Steph Barnes left Des for.

9. What are the names of the two men Tanya Pooley had affairs with during 1994?

10. Who did Ken Barlow begin an affair with in 1994?

Answers on p. 116

1. Name this character and his brother.

2. Name the actors.

3. What are the characters' dates of birth?

4. How much money did Steve McDonald borrow from his mum Liz in June 1994?

5. Which university did Andy go to for a short while?

6. Which of the twins rented the flat above Jim's Café?

7. In 1994 what did Steve develop a passion for?

8. Which twin was Vicki Alden sweet on?

9. Who planned to marry Amy Nelson?

10. Which twin went into the T-shirt business in 1994?

Answers on p. 117

Family Fortunes (10): The McDonald Family

1. What is the name of Jim McDonald's mother?

2. What was Andy's fiancé's name?

3. Which McDonald man punched brewery boss Richard Willmore?

4. What business did Jim run under the arches?

5. Who did Liz McDonald have an affair with in 1993?

6. Who employed Steve McDonald in February 1993?

7. How much compensation did Liz receive from Newton and Ridley?

8. What was Liz's job when she first worked at the Rovers?

9. In the summer of 1991 Jim arranged a night-fishing trip. Name the men who went.

10. Who has Jim worked for since 1993?

Answers on p. 116

1. Who is this character?

2. Name the actress who plays her.

3. Where did she take a holiday in the summer of 1994?

4. Who did she go with?

5. Name her first husband.

6. Who is her best friend in the Street?

7. Who tried to kill her?

8. How many times has she been married?

9. Which male resident of the Street has a soft spot for her?

10. How much money did she give to Sally and Kevin Webster?

Answers on p. 117

SECTION THREE:
Coronation Street

MASTERCLASS

Early Days

1. Who appeared in *Coronation Street* for 23 years and holds a *Guinness Book of Records* entry for his 76-year career on stage and TV which began in 1907?

2. What were the surnames of the three Harrys who set the series up in 1960?

3. Who was the Irish actor who played a tailor in *Never Mind the Quality, Feel the Width*, and a taxi driver friend of Elsie Tanner's in *Coronation Street*?

4. Who accused Elsie Lappin of selling her a 'rotten egg' and demanded a replacement in Episode One?

5. Where did Albert Tatlock win his First World War Military Medal on the Somme?

6. What were the names given to the Barlow twins born in 1965?

7. Which actor failed to land the role of Dennis Tanner in 1960 but popped up as an occasional Street Jack-the-Lad for the next twenty years?

8. Who protested loudly in 1961 because his father came to the dinner table without his collar and tie on?

9. What was the name of the now demolished Salford street that was the design prototype for Coronation Street?

10. Where did Tony Warren find the legend 'Florizel' the early name for *Coronation Street*?

Answers on p. 118

The Sizzling Seventies

1. When Len and Rita Fairclough married on 20 April 1977, who was Len's best man?

2. In 1976, whose coat did Bet Lynch give away in The Rover's for a Bonfire Night Guy?

3. List three members of the four-strong Hopkins family who took over the Corner Shop from Maggie Clegg in 1974?

4. When The Rover's was evacuated because of a fire at the warehouse opposite in 1975, and Annie Walker lost her leather bag, what was in it?

5. Why did the *Weatherfield Gazette* readers raise £600 for Hilda Ogden in 1970?

6. Ken Barlow proposed marriage to a hotel receptionist in 1971, but she turned him down. What was her name?

7. After Emily and Ernest Bishop's marriage on Easter Monday in 1972, where did they honeymoon?

8. Who won the beer drinking contest against Piggy Owen of the Flying Horse at the Weatherfield Pub Olympics in 1972?

9. Who ended up in Guy's Hospital, London, after being knocked down by a taxi in 1973?

10. Which Street babe was involved when a lorry ploughed into The Rover's Return in 1979?

Answers on p. 118

The Last Decade

1. Which Street actress was voted Britain's fourth most popular person – behind the Queen, the Queen Mother, and Princess Diana?

2. Which Salford MP took to calling himself 'the member for Coronation Street?

3. The unlikeliest soap wedding of any year took place in September 1988. Who were the bride and groom?

4. Why did Stan Ogden have to sell his window-cleaning round in March 1983?

5. Why did Mavis Riley's driving test joy turn into misery in June 1984?

6. What caused the bitter feud between neighbours the Duckworths and the Claytons in May 1985?

7. Who returned to terrorise Emily Bishop in 1981 and ended up in a mental home?

8. Who died in a car accident at Christmas, 1983, after a night out with another woman?

9. What special anniversary did *Coronation Street* celebrate in June 1980?

10. Which cast member received the MBE in the 1983 New Year's Honours List?

Answers on p. 118

Replay '89

1. In January 1989, who perpetrated a fraud in the name of a dead man?

2. Which single-parent battered wife joined the Street cast of characters in February 1989?

3. What is the name of the man who bought Brian Tilsley's garage?

4. Who led Jack Duckworth a dance, and took his wallet for a ride in April 1989?

5. What was the name of the pensioner 'gigolo' who made a play for Emily Bishop?

6. Who was the 'sheik of Weatherfield' who returned from the desert bearing gifts in May 1989?

7. Who gave a greyhound to Don Brennan in lieu of a taxi fare?

8. Who was the brewery marketing manager who was tapped up by Jack Duckworth in June 1989?

9. What was the name of the town hall 'mole' who was feeding information to the *Weatherfield Recorder*?

10. Who was the property developer who enticed Mike Baldwin to sell his garment factory in August 1989?

Answers on p. 118

The Nineties

1. What was the name of the long-lost daughter whom Alec Gilroy got in touch with in 1990?

2. Name the builder Tina Fowler was seeing during 1990.

3. In March 1990 what did Ken Barlow have to sell to help pay off his mortgage?

4. What medical condition did Alf Roberts contract in January 1994?

5. Who took Bet to the 1994 Licensed Victuallers' Ball?

6. How much did Jeff and Doreen Horton (Lisa Duckworth's parents) pay Terry for the baby Tommy during Christmas 1993?

7. Who was made Mayor of Weatherfield in May 1994?

8. In September 1991 who did Alf employ to work at the Corner Shop?

9. How much did Curly pay Rita for Number 7 in the summer of 1992?

10. Name the vegetable Mavis gave Derek to pep up their love life.

Answers on p. 119

Champion's Tie-breaker

If you've tackled this quiz in competition with others – here is your last chance to find the champion.

1. Who was debagged by factory girls at Christmas in 1976 because he refused to switch pay day to Thursdays?

2. What was the name of The Kabin newagents before Len Fairclough changed the name in 1973?

3. Which TV mogul, and major ITV company, refused to transmit *Coronation Street* when it first began?

4. Which new Street producer axed a host of early popular characters including Martha Longhurst?

5. Which well-known Street actress threatened to smack Tony Warren's bottom when he was twelve because he wouldn't keep quiet?

6. How did Hilda Ogden celebrate her 49th birthday in 1973?

7. What was the name of the sailing boat that Jerry Booth built in Len Fairclough's yard in 1972?

8. Who was jailed in Walton Prison for overstaying his parole at Christmas 1975?

9. Which British army regiment adopted Pat Phoenix as its pin-up in 1962?

10. What are the names of the three child actresses who have portrayed Tracey Barlow over a decade?

Answers on p. 119

SECTION FOUR:
Coronation Street

35th ANNIVERSARY

December 9th 1960 is one of the most memorable dates in television history, as Coronation Street was born. This section is dedicated to thirty-five years of the programme; there are some tricky Street teasers for all you die-hard fans who have mastered this book.

Now thinking caps on.

1. Which resident of Coronation Street is left-handed?

2. Who said of Elsie Tanner "She thinks that everything in trousers is for her, from boy scouts upwards"?

3. Which Street resident had a telephone installed in December 1965?

4. In 1980 Martin Cheveski had an autumn romance with whom?

5. Which woman from the old days was an artists' model?

6. Who said of Hilda Ogden "In darkest Africa they use a set of drums, here we've got Hilda Ogden. I suppose that's civilisation"?

7. Whose birthday is on 1st December?

8. In 1964 Stan Ogden had a job as a chauffeur for which company?

9. Name the Alsatian dog Eddie Yeats and Stan Ogden bought in 1975.

10. What did Stan and Hilda have over their bed?

Answers on page 120

35 Years (2)

1. In 1976 Hilda won a trolley dash at the local delicatessen. Who helped her?

2. In 1971, Irma Ogden had an affair with a top professional footballer. What was his name?

3. Name the two Street characters who share their birthday on 3rd September.

4. Who was 21 on 26th June 1995?

5. What name did Liz McDonald give her baby, who died after a few days, in 1992?

6. What was the name of the baby Andrea Clayton had by Terry Duckworth?

7. Name Betty Turpin's daughter-in-law.

8. What was Alma's nick-name for Maggie Redman?

9. How old was Vicki when her parents died?

10. In 1992, Bet introduced a Happy Hour at the Rovers. Between which hours?

Answers on page 120

1. At the 1969 Rovers Christmas party, Minnie Caldwell recited which famous poem?

2. At Christmas in 1984, Percy Sugden did impressions for the regulars at the Rovers. What were they of?

3. Name Sandra Stubbs' violent husband.

4. When did Raquel join the Rovers' staff?

5. In 1992 the Rovers kitchens underwent a revamp. How much did it cost Alec Gilroy?

6. In 1990 Bet and Alec were offered another pub. What was its name?

7. In which year did Betty first make her now famous hot pot for the Rovers?

8. Where did Annie Walker spend the last few years?

9. Name Alec Gilroy's first wife.

10. Who upset Ena Sharples in September 1961 by playing a radio behind the bar of the Rovers?

Answers on page 120

35 Years (4)

1. In 1964 Irma Ogden started work at the Rovers, and was sacked on her first night. Why?

2. Name Gloria Todd's ex-boyfriend and former prisoner.

3. Which brewery competition did Annie win in 1969?

4. What did Deirdre's mum, Blanche Hunt, make?

5. In 1981 Annie Walker set off on a three week cruise. Where was her destination?

6. What date did the new look Rovers open after the fire in 1986?

7. Name the two characters who share a birthday on 18th October.

8. Name Maggie Redmond's first husband.

9. What was Maureen Holdsworth's surname before she married Reg?

10. Name Betty Turpin's grandson.

Answers on page 120

1. What road is Bettabuys on?

2. What is Liz McDonald's maiden name?

3. When, and in which church, did Jim and Liz McDonald marry?

4. How much did Mike Baldwin pay for his Docklands flat?

5. What was the name of Don Brennan's first wife?

6. What was Derek's mother's name?

7. Name the owner of the larger mini-market on Rosamond Street.

8. What was Phyllis Pearce's husband's name?

9. What year did Alma and Jim Sedgwick's marriage break up?

10. What is the address of Alma and Jim's Cafe?

Answers on page 121

1. How much did Gail and Martin pay for their house – the most expensive in the street?

2. What was Betty Turpin's maiden name?

3. What was Ivy Brennan's maiden name?

4. What was Bert Tilsley's full name?

5. Which road is Weatherfield General Hospital on?

6. Name the church that Ivy often visited.

7. Which 1970's blonde resident once demonstrated German sausages in the local supermarket?

8. What did Reg Holdsworth's father do for a living?

9. Name Phyllis Pearce's daughter.

10. When is Tracy Barlow's birthday?

Answers on page 121

ANSWERS

Section One:
Coronation Street Starters

People . . .

1. (c) Tony Warren. 2. (b) Three. 3. (c) Jack Walker.
4. (c) Dennis. 5. (c) Newton and Ridley.
6. (c) Sonny Jim. 7. (c) Concepta Riley.
8. (c) Albert Tatlock. 9. (c) Gunshot wounds.
10. (b) Gin and tonic.

. . . and Places

1. (c) Weatherfield. 2. (b) The Kabin. 3. (a) Salford.
4. (a) St Annes on Sea. 5. (d) Australia.
6. (c) Lisbon. 7. (b) Inkerman Street.
8. (a) Bessie Street. 9. (a) Canada.
10. (b) The Somme.

First Cast . . .

1. (a) Wilfred Pickle's pianist. 2. (d) Maudie Edwards.
3. (b) Arthur Leslie. 4. (b) Margot Bryant.
5. (c) Susan Jamieson. 6. (c) Austrian. 7. (a) Ireland.
8. (b) Angela Douglas. 9. (c) Mrs Dale's Diary.
10. (c) Ivan Beavis.

Star Quotes

1. (b) Ken Irwin. 2. (c) Russell Harty.
3. (a) The Queen. 4. (c) Harold Wilson.
5. (a) John Betjeman. 6. (c) Tony Warren.
7. (a) Cyril Smith. 8. (b) Bill Podmore.
9. (c) James Callaghan. 10. (a) Ken Irwin.

Deaths and Disasters

1. (b) Martha Longhurst. 2. (d) Ena Sharples.
3. (a) Ida Barlow. 4. (c) Maggie Clegg.
5. (b) Betty Turpin's. 6. (c) Harry Hewitt.
7. (c) Joe Donnelli. 8. (d) Phyllis. 9. (b) Stan Ogden.
10. (b) Ena Sharples'.

Which Year?

1. (a) 1963. 2. (c) 1986. 3. (c) 1987. 4. (d) 1971.
5. (b) 1971. 6. (c) 1983. 7. (a) 1983. 8. (c) 1988.
9. (b) 1989. 10. (c) 1961.

Fleeting Faces

1. (b) Max Wall. 2. (c) Herman of the Hermits.
3. (c) Richard Beckinsale. 4. (a) Davey Jones.
5. (c) Bill Maynard. 6. (b) Joanna Lumley.
7. (a) Mollie Sugden. 8. (c) Ben Kingsley.
9. (b) Prunella Scales. 10. (a) Martin Shaw.

Whose baby?

1. (c) Paul Cheveski. 2. (a) Christopher Hewitt.
3. (b) Ken Barlow's. 4. (c) Irma Barlow.
5. (b) Ray Langton. 6. (a) Gail Tilsley.
7. (c) Betty Turpin's. 8. (c) Hilda Ogden's
9. (a) Bet Lynch. 10. (c) Sarah Louise.

Rogues' Gallery

1. (a) Kenneth Cope. 2. (d) Ena Sharples.
3. (b) Albert Tatlock. 4. (c) Emily Nugent.
5. (c) Valerie Barlow. 6. (a) Elsie Tanner.
7. (b) Arnold Swain. 8. (d) The Duckworths.
9. (c) Ena Sharples. 10. (c) They got life imprisonment.

True or False?

1. True and, like her brother, Lynne worked as a stand-up comedienne in cabaret before she turned to acting.

2. True. And Elsie had 20 boy-friends too during her 22-year reign as Queen of the Street.

3. True. But the producers thought it sounded too much like a disinfectant and changed the name before its first screening.

4. False.

5. True. Her father is Lord Harmer-Nicholls, the former Tory MP whose county seat is in Cheshire.

6. True. Bill never intended to stay this long but reckons, 'I have been very comfortable and the years have just rolled by'.

7. False. The Street has been toppled in the ratings many times by shows like *Dad's Army*, and mainly by the now deposed 1980s leader *EastEnders*.

8. True. He played Gorden Clegg, but tried his hand successfully at theatre management and gradually slipped out of acting.

9. False. Warren was born a few miles away across the River Irwell boundary in Salford where the programme is set.

10. True. Bernard was a velvet-voiced announcer working alongside the BBC's Ray Moore, long before he played gruff Stan.

Street Speak

1. (d) Look who's here! **2.** (b) A fool. **3.** (a) Always.
4. (c) Hungry. **5.** (d) Outdoor toilet. **6.** (a) Puzzled.
7. (b) Alleyway. **8.** (b) Bad tempered. **9.** (b) Died.
10. Bread soaked in warm milk.

Stars of Song

1. (c) The Orinoco Club.   2. (b) Harmonium.
3. (c) Vince St Clair.   4. (c) Stephen Hancock.
5. (a) Bill Waddington.   6. (c) Betty Driver.
7. (b) Vera and Ivy.   8. (b) Alec Gilroy.
9. (c) Betty, Bet and Norma.   10. (d) Dennis Tanner.

Funny Men!

1. (a) Chalkie Whiteley.   2. (c) A sea-lion.
3. (c) She cut up all his trousers.   4. (a) Roy Barraclough.
5. (b) Resident comic.   6. (c) CB radio.
7. (c) Alec Gilroy.   8. (b) Percy Sugden.
9. (a) Len Fairclough.   10. (b) Stan Odgen.

A barmaid's lot!

1. (c) Bet Lynch.   2. (a) Betty Turpin.
3. (b) Concepta Riley.   4. (b) Gloria Todd.
5. (c) Eunice Nuttall.   6. (a) Sandra Stubbs.
7. (b) Suzie Birchall.   8. (b) Tina Fowler.
9. (a) Megan Morgan.   10. (c) Betty Turpin.

Animal Magic!

1. (b) Don Brennan.   2. (d) Bill Waddington.
3. (c) Sharon Gaskell.   4. (b) The cat on the roof in the
opening titles.   5. (a) Fred Gee.   6. (b) Tommy Deakin.
7. (c) Minnie Caldwell.   8. (b) Made it a member of their
union.   9. (a) It was stolen by thieves.
10. (d) Albert Tatlock.

Sons and Daughters

1. (c) Trevor.   2. (a) Jenny.   3. (c) Terry.
4. (b) Nicky.   5. (b) The Bishops.
6. (c) Ivy Brennan's.   7. (a) Lucille Hewitt.
8. (d) Susan.   9. (c) Gail Tilsley's.
10. (b) Valerie Barlow.

Occupations

1. (b) A window-cleaning business.
2. (c) GPO supervisor.   3. (c) Car mechanic.
4. (a) Italian restaurant.   5. (b) Betting shop.
6. (a) Fred Gee.   7. (c) Rag-and-bone man.
8. (c) Sally Waterman.   9. (d) Balloons and novelties.
10. (b) Elsie Lappin.

Funny Girls!

1. (a) Hilda Ogden.   2. (c) Vera Duckworth.
3. (a) Audrey Roberts.   4. (b) Amanda Barrie.
5. (b) Marion Willis.   6. (a) Jill Summers.
7. (a) Ena Sharples.   8. (c) Hilda Ogden.
9. (d) Annie Walker.   10. (b) Lucille Hewitt.

Men in Uniform

1. (b) Percy Sugden.   2. (a) William Roache.
3. (b) Terry Duckworth.   4. (c) Len Fairclough.
5. (d) Bill Gregory.   6. (c) Albert Tatlock.
7. (b) Gregg Flint.   8. (c) A bugler.
9. (a) Elsie Tanner's.   10. (c) Arthur Lowe.

Neighbours

1. (c) The Barlows.   2. (b) The Duckworths.
3. (b) Mavis Wilton.   4. (b) Number 13.
5. (a) May and Christine Hardman.
6. (c) The Glad Tidings Mission.   7. (b) Inkerman Street.
8. (b) Hopkins.   9. (a) Number 7.
10. (c) Mike Baldwin.

Gone But Not Forgotten

1. Ireland   2. He shaved Kevin's moustache at the Barnes' house-warming party.   3. Debi Scott   4. Builder and decorator.   5. 35 years old.   6. Mexico.   7. Trinidad.
8. Bar steward in the Merchant Navy.   9. Mitzi.
10. 28 years old.

The Youth Of The Nineties

1. Nicky Platt.   2. The garage where Kevin Webster was manager and Mark was the trainee.   3. France.
4. France.   5. The dentist Robert Weston.   6. Weatherfield Comprehensive.   7. Carmel Finnan.   8. Des Barnes and Curly Watts.   9. Oakhill Grammar.   10. Craig.

Cross The Road

1. Maurice Jones.   2. Maurice Jones.   3. Emily Bishop and Deirdre Barlow.   4. Des and Stephanie Barnes.   5. Rita Sullivan.   6. A charity shop selling second hand clothes for the hospital.   7. Mavis and Derek Wilton.   8. Denise's Salon.   9. Denise Osbourne.   10. Fiona Middleton.

Weddings in the Nineties

1. Maggie Redman (Mike's old girlfriend).   2. 17 Elmgate Gardens, Weatherfield.   3. £50,000.   4. 19th June 1992.
5. Deirdre Barlow.   6. Terry Duckworth ran off, as he had been let out of prison for the day to marry Lisa.   7. Curly Watts.   8. In Charlie's rig.   9. Confectionery salesman for Cartwrights.   10. Derek Wilton. He thought that Ted was after Rita's money and didn't know Ted was dying.

Section Two:
Coronation Street Addicts

Happy Families

1. Valerie Barlow's.　2. Stanley.　3. Bet Lynch.
4. Trevor Ogden.　5. Gina Seddon.
6. Damian and Jane.　7. Amy Barton.　8. Potter.
9. Ken Barlow.　10. Frank.　11. Harry Bailey.
12. Jason.　13. Billy Walker's.　14. Elsie Tanner's.
15. Ian Latimer, Brian's Australian cousin.

Wedding Bells

1. Jack Duckworth.　2. Gloria Todd.
3. Mavis Riley and Derek Wilton.
4. Irene Sherratt and Sandra Pilkington.
5. Marion was pregnant.
6. Tracey Langton and Susan Barlow.　7. Eunice Nuttall.
8. Rita Littlewood.　9. Valerie Tatlock.
10. Benny Lewis.　11. Pat Phoenix and Alan Browning.
12. Harry Hewitt died in an accident.　13. Ken Barlow.
14. Mavis Riley.　15. Her father Jack Walker.

Drink to Me Only . . .

1. Port and lemon and Planter's Punch.
2. Jack Duckworth and Mike Baldwin.
3. Her husband Alan.　4. A double rum.
5. The Flying Horse.　6. Kath Goodwin.
7. Frank Harvey.　8. Fred Gee.　9. Gordon Lewis.
10. A lorry ploughed into the pub.　11. Betty Turpin.
12. Minnie Caldwell and Emily Nugent.
13. Linda and Ivan Cheveski.　14. The Mechanic's Arms.
15. Tanya.

Action Replay (1)

1. Sally Webster.　2. She took up car 'banger' racing.
3. A broken leg.　4. Kevin.　5. Gina.
6. Alf's Mini Market.　7. Seddon.　8. Hilda Ogden.
9. Number 13.　10. 1986.

Family Fortunes (1): The Ogdens

1. Crabtree.   2. Clairvoyance.   3. Henry Wakefield.
4. Lorry driver.   5. The woman at 19 Inkerman Street.
6. A partnership in the Corner Shop.   7. Eddie Yeats.
8. They were a wedding gift from Aunt Aggie.
9. Bet Gilroy and Mike Baldwin.   10. Dr Lowther.
11. She was mugged.   12. Tom Hopwood.
13. 'The greatest living Englishman'.   14. A 'glass' back.
15. Bernard Youens and Jean Alexander.

Family Favourites

1. The Ogdens and the Hopkins.   2. Ken Barlow.
3. The Hopkins.   4. The Tilsleys.
5. The Brennans and the Duckworths.   6. The Gilroys.
7. The Websters.   8. The Barlows and the Baldwins.
9. The Walkers.   10. The Websters.
11. The Cheveskis.   12. The Tilsleys.
13. The Bonartis.   14. The Gilroys.   15. The Barlows.

The Young Ones

1. Jenny Bradley.   2. Curly Watts.
3. Kevin Kennedy who plays Curly Watts.
4. Terry Duckworth.   5. Gina Seddon.
6. The Websters.   7. Ena Sharples.   8. Brian Tilsley.
9. The Faircloughs.   10. Lucille Hewitt.
11. Elsie Tanner's.   12. Suzie Birchall.
13. Kevin Webster.   14. Andrea Clayton.
15. Tina Fowler.

Action Replay (2)

1. Eileen Derbyshire.   2. Emily Nugent.
3. She failed to turn up at church.
4. She proposed – it was Leap Year.
5. Leonard Swindley.   6. Twice (once bigamously).
7. Bigamist Arnold Swain.   8. Baldwin's factory office.
9. Valerie Barlow.
10. She was electrocuted in an accident.

Laughter Makers

1. Percy Sugden. 2. Bill Waddington.
3. Hilda Ogden's. 4. Geoffrey Hughes.
5. Hilda Ogden. 6. Jack Duckworth.
7. Vera Duckworth and Ivy Tilsley. 8. Irma Barlow.
9. Fred Gee and Eddie Yeats. 10. Nora Batty.
11. Annie Walker's. 12. Arthur Lowe.
13. Mavis Riley's. 14. Annie Walker.
15. Stan Ogden.

Family Fortunes (2): The Barlows

1. Two. 2. Ida. 3. Kenneth. 4. David.
5. Since Episode One. 6. William Roache. 7. Three.
8. Valerie. 9. Mike Baldwin. 10. Susan.
11. Alf Roberts. 12. Tracey. 13. School teacher.
14. Eddie Yeats. 15. Irma Ogden.

Guys and Dolls

1. Stan Ogden. 2. Sonia Price. 3. Billy Gregory.
4. Rita Littlewood. 5. Craig. 6. Gail Tilsley.
7. Ray Langton. 8. Bet Lynch. 9. Frank Barlow.
10. Emily Nugent. 11. Alan Howard's.
12. Elsie Tanner. 13. Percy Sugden.
14. Andrea Clayton. 15. Victor Pendlebury.

Action Replay (3)

1. Peter Baldwin. 2. Derek Wilton. 3. Mavis.
4. Over The Kabin. 5. He lost his job. 6. His mother.
7. Victor Pendlebury. 8. Making toy theatres.
9. His sister. 10. A moon-stone ring.

Find the Surnames

1. Gilroy, née Lynch. 2. (Eddie) Yeats.
3. (Alf) Roberts. 4. (Ray) Langton.
5. (Len) Fairclough. 6. Barlow. 7. Matthews.
8. Tilsley. 9. (Bill) Tarmey. 10. (Betty) Turpin.
11. (Tony) Warren. 12. Willis. 13. Lappin.
14. Potts. 15. (Annie) Walker.

Senior Citizens

1. Elsie Lappin. 2. A hairnet. 3. Phyllis Pearce.
4. Sam Tindall. 5. Percy Sugden. 6. Minnie Caldwell.
7. Sonny Jim. 8. Martha Longhurst. 9. Ena Sharples.
10. Albert Tatlock. 11. Tom Hopwood.
12. Len Marten. 13. Sam Tindall. 14. Tom Mennard.
15. Jack Howarth.

Family Fortunes (3): The Tilsleys

1. Ivy and Bert. 2. Filling station attendant.
3. He beat up a young robber. 4. 1979. 5. Potter.
6. In Len Fairclough's new house. 7. Les Charlton.
8. A garage. 9. Her husband died in hospital.
10. Lynne Perrie. 11. Brennan.
12. George Hepworth. 13. Threw him out.
14. Classical music and astronomy. 15. Tricia Hopkins.

Action Replay (4)

1. Helen Worth. 2. Gail Tilsley.
3. Her husband was stabbed to death. 4. Nicky.
5. Sarah Louise. 6. Alf Roberts. 7. Ian Latimer.
8. Martin Platt. 9. A garage.
10. Her mum was an unmarried mother.

Trade Marks

1. Alf Roberts. 2. Hilda Ogden. 3. Eddie Yeats.
4. Stan Ogden. 5. Albert Tatlock. 6. Ena Sharples.
7. Bet Lynch. 8. Phyllis Pearce. 9. Vera Duckworth.
10. Brian Tilsley. 11. Elsie Tanner.
12. Mike Baldwin. 13. Deirdre Barlow.
14. Ivy Brennan. 15. Mavis Wilton.

Jumbled Names

1. Ken Barlow. 2. Len Fairclough. 3. Ena Sharples.
4. Mike Baldwin. 5. Eddie Yeats. 6. Elsie Tanner.
7. Albert Tatlock. 8. Gail Tilsley.
9. Vera Duckworth. 10. Jed Stone.
11. Leonard Swindley. 12. Martha Longhurst.
13. Bet Gilroy. 14. Suzie Birchall. 15. Annie Walker.

Coronation Street Egg Heads

1. Ken Barlow. 2. Curly Watts. 3. Jenny Bradley.
4. Ernest Bishop. 5. Gordon Clegg. 6. Annie Walker.
7. Curly Watts. 8. Ken Barlow. 9. Esther Hayes.
10. Elsie Tanner. 11. Wilfred Perkins.
12. Mavis Riley. 13. Mavis Riley.
14. Bill Roache once served as an army officer in charge of Bedouin tribesmen. 15. Percy Sugden.

Action Replay (5)

1. Jack Howarth. 2. Albert Tatlock. 3. Alice Pickens.
4. Their wedding has just been postponed.
5. The Lancashire Fusiliers. 6. Valerie Barlow.
7. Beattie. 8. *Number 1*. 9. Clara Midgeley.
10. Lollipop man.

Family Fortunes (4): The Tanners

1. Arnold Tanner.   2. Two.   3. Patricia Phoenix.
4. Portugal.   5. Dennis.   6. Ladies' hairdressing.
7. Ricky Dennis.   8. Breaking and entering.   9. Linda.
10. Steve.   11. American.   12. Army master sergeant.
13. He died falling down stairs.   14. 1986.
15. Actor Tony Booth.

Nick Names

1. Stan Ogden.   2. Bernard Youens.   3. Norman.
4. Jed Stone.   5. Eddie Yeats.   6. Brett Falcon.
7. Jack Duckworth.   8. Chalkie.   9. Eddie Yeats'.
10. Jack Duckworth.   11. Elsie Tanner.
12. Stan Ogden District Union.
13. The Irish comic at the Orinoco Club.
14. Charlie Moffitt.   15. La Composita.

Forgotten Stars

1. Elsie Lappin.   2. Mr Swindley.   3. Alice Pickens.
4. Arthur Stokes.   5. 'Fangio' Bateman.
6. Dave Smith.   7. Fred Clark.   8. Himself.
9. Cyril Turpin.   10. Norman Crabtree.
11. Alma Sedgewick.   12. Monica Sutton.
13. Sir Julius Berlin.   14. Bill Gregory.
15. George Barton.

Action Replay (6)

1. Anne Kirkbride.   2. Deirdre Barlow.
3. Town councillor.   4. Mike Baldwin.
5. Ray Langton.   6. Newspaper editor.   7. Tracey.
8. Len Fairclough.
9. She thought Tracey had been killed.   10. Spectacles.

Trouble Makers

1. Mike Baldwin. **2.** Arnold Swain. **3.** Alan Bradley.
4. His wife Myra. **5.** Neil Crossley. **6.** Mike Baldwin.
7. Her ex-husband. **8.** Ian Latimer.
9. Terry Duckworth. **10.** Eddie Yeats's.
11. Len Fairclough. **12.** Elsie Tanner.
13. Ray Langton. **14.** Her son Billy.
15. Emily Bishop's.

Sick Parade

1. Ena Sharples. **2.** Robert Maxwell.
3. David Barlow's. **4.** Ena Sharples' daughter Vera.
5. Albert Tatlock. **6.** Stan Ogden.
7. She had been mugged. **8.** Bet Lynch.
9. Albert Tatlock. **10.** Stan Ogden. **11.** Bert Tilsley.
12. Hilda Ogden. **13.** Ray Langton.
14. She opted for an abortion.
15. Stephen Reid, her adopted son.

Family Favourites (5): The Faircloughs

1. They were killed in an air-raid.
2. In the Royal Navy on Russian convoys. **3.** Bricklayer.
4. 15 Mawdsley Street. **5.** Elsie Tanner.
6. Ken Barlow's. **7.** The taxi had a flat tyre.
8. As a singer in third-rate revues.
9. At a school parents' meeting.
10. She thought Len had been unfaithful.
11. Sharon Gaskell. **12.** Jenny Bradley.
13. Tony Cunliffe. **14.** Mavis Wilton.
15. Alf Roberts.

Action Replay (7)

1. Mark Eden. **2.** Alan Bradley. **3.** Rita Fairclough.
4. Embezzle her savings. **5.** Len Fairclough's.
6. Weatherfield Security Systems. **7.** Martin Platt.
8. Dawn Prescott. **9.** Jenny Bradley. **10.** Sue Nicholls.

Cars of the Stars

1. The Websters.   2. A bus.   3. A Jaguar.
4. A Rover 2000 saloon.   5. A taxi.   6. A lorry.
7. Chauffeuring.   8. Emily Nugent.
9. It had faulty steering.   10. Billy Walker.
11. Alan Howard.   12. Renée Roberts.
13. Eddie Yeats.   14. George Wardle.
15. Ken Barlow.

Blonde Bombshells

1. Ivy Brennan and Vera Duckworth.   2. Annie Walker.
3. Brian Tilsley.   4. Bet Lynch.   5. Len Fairclough.
6. His wife Audrey.   7. Tina Fowler.
8. Deirdre Barlow.   9. Eunice Nuttall.
10. Mavis Riley.   11. Maggie Clegg.
12. Yvonne Chapel.   13. Gail Tilsley.
14. Hilda Ogden.   15. Jenny.

The Fugitives

1. Gorden Clegg and Lucille Hewitt.   2. The Hopkins.
3. Terry Duckworth.   4. Suzie Birchall.
5. Sheila Birtles.   6. Minnie Caldwell.
7. Maggie Clegg.   8. Alan Bradley.   9. Fred Gee.
10. Bill Gregory and Elsie Tanner.   11. Concepta Hewitt.
12. Alan Howard.   13. Dave Smith and Blanche Hunt.
14. Ray Langton.   15. Canada.

Action Replay (8)

1. Bill Tarmey and Elizabeth Dawn.
2. Jack and Vera Duckworth.   3. Terry.
4. He took barmaid Tina Fowler on a night out.
5. Ivy Brennan.   6. Baldwin's Garment Factory.
7. Alec Gilroy.   8. Number 9.   9. The Clayton's.
10. Selling jeans.

Family Fortunes (6): The Websters

1. Bill. 2. Debbie. 3. Property repair man.
4. Southampton. 5. Kevin. 6. Sally Seddon.
7. Brian Tilsley's garage. 8. He was murdered.
9. Alf Robert's Mini Market. 10. Number 13.
11. Hilda Ogden. 12. Gina Seddon.
13. Michael le Vell. 14. Sally Whittaker.
15. Percy Sugden's niece Elaine.

Pot Pourri

1. Jerry Booth's. 2. Ernest Bishop. 3. Mavis Riley.
4. Albert Tatlock. 5. Maurice Jones.
6. Percy Sugden. 7. Derek Wilton.
8. Bernie Bagshaw. 9. *EastEnders. Coronation Street*
officially reclaimed its place at the top of the ratings again
in January 1989, when Granada started a Sunday Omnibus
repeat to match *EastEnders*. 10. His wife Audrey.
11. Chalkie Whiteley. 12. Bet Lynch.
13. Jack Duckworth. 14. Tom Hopwood.
15. Elsie Tanner.

Family Fortunes (7): The Walkers

1. Annie. 2. Joan. 3. Deirdre Langton. 4. Jersey.
5. 1970. 6. Arthur Leslie.
7. Because Leslie had died suddenly. 8. Derby.
9. Annie Walker. 10. Her work in a cotton mill.
11. Mayoress of Weatherfield. 12. Fred Gee.
13. Betty Turpin. 14. 1983.
15. With her daughter Joan.

Action Replay (9)

1. Bryan Mosley. 2. Alf Roberts.
3. The Street mini market. 4. Audrey. 5. Phyllis.
6. Renée Bradshaw. 7. The Post Office.
8. Rita Littlewood. 9. Deirdre Barlow.
10. The Royal Corp of Signals.

Family Fortunes (8): The Claytons

1. Four. 2. Harry, Connie, Andrea and Sue. 3. 1985.
4. Number 11. 5. The Websters. 6. The Duckworths.
7. Andrea. 8. Dressmaker. 9. Played the trombone.
10. Johnny Leeze. 11. Susan Brown. 12. Andrea.
13. She turned him down. 14. Elsie Tanner. 15. 1987.

Food for Thought

1. Percy Sugden. 2. Barm Cakes. 3. Hilda Ogden's.
4. Alma Sedgewick and Gail Tilsley. 5. Albert Tatlock.
6. Alf Roberts. 7. Ena Sharples. 8. Stan Ogden.
9. Lionel Petty. 10. Stan Ogden.
11. Baldwin sold his garment factory. 12. Stan Ogden.
13. Percy Sugden. 14. Phyllis Pearce.
15. Deirdre Langton.

Family Fortunes (9): The Duckworths

1. Jack. 2. Ivy Brennan. 3. The abbatoir.
4. Choice cuts of meat. 5. William Tarmey.
6. Elizabeth Dawn. 7. Nigel Pivaro. 8. Alec Gilroy.
9. Curly Watts. 10. To take in a female lodger.
11. The Clothing Factory. 12. Mike Baldwin. 13. 1986.
14. £250. 15. Vera.

Action Replay (10)

1. Julie Goodyear. 2. Bet Gilroy née Lynch.
3. The Rover's Return. 4. Martin. 5. Billy Walker's.
6. 1985. 7. In a cafe in Spain. 8. Fred Gee.
9. Len Fairclough. 10. Ex-Borstal boy Frank Bradley.

Women Of The Nineties

1. The Pizza Hut, Weatherfield. 2. The spiritualist meetings
at the local spiritualist church. 3. Mac. 4. Dave Barton.
5. Mortgage manager Adrian Gosthorpe. 6. Rhos-on-sea.
7. Rachel. 8. Rosamund Caterers. 9. 47 Church Road,
Weatherfield. 10. Rita Sullivan.

Men Of The Nineties

1. PJ 1. 2. 9th October. 3. Vernon. 4. Southampton.
5. Ben Cunningham. 6. Brian Bowes. 7. Jack
Duckworth. 8. Ken Barlow. 9. Manager of a betting
shop. 10. Wayne Farrell.

Bettabuys

1. Renee Dodds. 2. Rita Fairclough. 3. Angie Freeman.
4. Lord 'Black Jack' Morgan. 5. Vanessa Morgan. 6. Vera
Duckworth. 7. Andy McDonald. 8. Monica. 9. Curly
(Norman) Watts. 10. Vera Duckworth.

Affairs Of The Nineties

1. Wendy Crozier. 2. Phil Jennings. 3. Des Barnes.
4. Joe Broughton. 5. Curly Watts. 6. Victor Pendlebury.
7. Paula Maxwell. 8. Simon Beattie. 9. Alex Christie and
Des Barnes. 10. Denise Osbourne.

Family Fortunes (10) The McDonald Family

1. Maisie. 2. Amy Nelson. 3. Jim McDonald. 4. A
motorbike repair business. 5. Colin Barnes (Des Barnes'
brother). 6. Mike Baldwin (In his T-shirt business).
7. £2,000. 8. Liz was employed to cook and serve the pub
meals in the evening. 9. Alf Roberts and Don Brennan.
10. Kevin Webster at MVB Motors (Mike Baldwin's repair
shop).

Action Replay (12)

1. Rita Sullivan. **2.** Barbara Knox. **3.** Blackpool. **4.** Sally, Kevin and Rosie Webster. **5.** Len Fairclough. **6.** Bet Gilroy. **7.** Alan Bradley. **8.** Twice: to Len Fairclough and Ted Sullivan. **9.** Alf Roberts. **10.** £5,000.

Action Replay (11)

1. Andy and Steve McDonald. **2.** Nicholas Cochrane and Simon Gregson. **3.** 26th June 1974. **4.** £500. **5.** Sheffield University. **6.** Andy. **7.** Betting on horse racing. **8.** Steve. **9.** Andy. **10.** Steve, working first for Mike Baldwin then for himself.

The Corner Shop In The Nineties

1. 7th February 1994. **2.** 8.30 am. **3.** Open it. **4.** Two months. **5.** Debi Scott. **6.** Brendan Scott. **7.** Deirdre Barlow and Emily Bishop. **8.** Alf Roberts. **9.** Ken Barlow. **10.** French lager illegally imported by Charlie Wheelan.

Reg, Maureen and Maud Too ...

1. Yellow roses. **2.** Paris. **3.** An antique brooch. **4.** Herne Bay. **5.** A water bed. **6.** Elizabeth. **7.** Martin Platt. **8.** Darjeeling. **9.** 26th January 1994. **10.** St. Christopher's, Weatherfield. The Belstaff Hotel.

Raquel

1. The Newton and Ridley 1995 calendar. **2.** Miss February 1995. **3.** Erik (The Flash) Mikaelson. **4.** Des Barnes. **5.** The photographer Ben Cunningham. **6.** Tanya Pooley. **7.** Wayne Farrell. **8.** Ken Barlow. **9.** Wayne Farrell. **10.** Mayfair Academy in Croydon.

Section Three:
Coronation Street Masterclass

Early Days

1. Jack Howarth.   2. Elton, Latham and Kershaw.
3. Joe Lynch.   4. Ena Sharples.   5. Vimmy Ridge.
6. Peter and Susan.
7. Kenneth Farrington (he played Billy Walker).
8. Ken Barlow.   9. Archie Street.
10. A 'Prince Charming' picture on his bedroom wall.

The Sizzling Seventies

1. Alf Roberts.   2. Hilda Ogden's.
3. Iris, Vera, Tricia and Granny.   4. 35 gold sovereigns.
5. To send her to Australia after a family car crash.
6. Yvonne Chapel.   7. Edale, Derbyshire.
8. Stan Ogden.   9. Elsie Tanner.   10. Tracey Langton.

The Last Decade

1. Jean Alexander.   2. Frank Allaun.
3. Bet Lynch and Alec Gilroy.
4. He got into debt with a moneylender.
5. She reversed into Jack Duckworth's taxi.
6. Vera refused to pay a £38 dress bill.   7. Arnold Swain.
8. Len Fairclough.   9. Its two thousandth episode.
10. Jack Howard

Replay '89

1. Alan Bradley.   2. Sandra Stubbs.   3. Tom Casey.
4. Barmaid Tina Fowler.   5. Arthur Dabner.
6. Alec Gilroy.   7. Harry Slinger.   8. Nigel Ridley.
9. Wendy Crozier.   10. Maurice Jones.

The Nineties

1. Sandra Arden. **2.** Eddie Ramsden. **3.** The Weatherfield Recorder. **4.** Gout. **5.** Charlie Wheelan. **6.** £5,000. **7.** Alf Roberts. **8.** Ivy Brennan. **9.** £30,000. **10.** Parsnips.

Champion's Tie-breaker

1. Ernest Bishop. **2.** Biddulphs'.
3. Lew Grade and ATV, Midlands. **4.** Tim Aspinall.
5. Violet Carson.
6. With a Barbara Cartland-style party. **7.** Shangri-La.
8. Eddie Yeats. **9.** King's Own Yorkshire Light Infantry.
10. Christabel Finch, Holly Chamarette, Dawn Acton.

Section Four

Coronation Street 35 Years (1)

1. William Roache or Ken Barlow.   **2.** Annie Walker.
3. Elsie Tanner.   **4.** Karen Oldfield.   **5.** Elsie Tanner.
6. Renne Roberts.   **7.** Denise Osburne.   **8.** Amalgamated
Steel.   **9.** Fury.   **10.** A sign which read "God Bless Our
Home".

Coronation Street 35 Years (2)

1. Deirdre Langton.   **2.** Eddie Duncan (played by Del
Henney).   **3.** Kevin Webster and Vera Duckworth.
4. Steve and Andy McDonald.   **5.** Katharine.
6. Paul.   **7.** Caroline.   **8.** Maggie Flower Shop.   **9.** 14 years
old.   **10.** The extended happy hour was 5pm to 6.30pm.

Coronation Street 35 Years (3)

1. The Owl and the Pussy Cat (she couldn't remember more
than the first verse).   **2.** Farmyard animal impressions (badly).
3. Ronnie Stubbs.   **4.** January 1992.   **5.** £7,000.   **6.** The
Quarryman's Rest.   **7.** 1973.   **8.** Derby.   **9.** Joyce Crosby.
10. Nona Willis.

Coronation Street 35 Years (4)

1. She dropped Annie's Willow pattern plate, smashing it to
pieces.   **2.** Steve Holt.   **3.** Most Popular Newton and Ridley
Land Lady.   **4.** Corsets.   **5.** Casablanca.   **6.** 13 August 1986.
7. Emily Bishop and Alma Baldwin.   **8.** Harry Redmond.
9. Naylor.   **10.** Peter.

Coronation Street 35 Years (5)

1. Albert Road. **2.** Greenwood. **3.** 5th January 1974 at St
Thomas' Church. **4.** £65,000. **5.** Pat. **6.** Amy Wilton.
7. Rajiv Patel. **8.** Harold. **9.** 1982. **10.** 12, Rosamond
Street, Weatherfield.

Coronation Street 35 Years (6)

1. £38,000. **2.** Preston. **3.** Nelson. **4.** Herbert Harrison
Tilsley. **5.** Curzon Street. **6.** St Luke's. **7.** Suzie Birchell.
8. He was a grocer. **9.** Margaret. **10.** 24th January.

ABOUT THE AUTHORS

Chris Stacey has watched *Coronation Street* since he was four years old and his earliest memory of the show is the 1964 Christmas Panto.

Now the country's top soap expert, Chris has written four other books for Boxtree: *Supersoaps* and the *Supersoaps Quizbooks 1, 2* and *3*. He is also often busy writing articles for the national press, most notably "The A-Z of Soaps", which he produced for the *News of The World*'s *Sunday* magazine.

Recently Chris presented cable channel WIRE TV's *Soap On The Wire* programme with co-presenter Femi Oki, and previously presented BSB's Galaxy Channel show, *31 West*. He regularly writes a page for *Cable Guide* and is often called in as soap expert for LBC and BBC Radio Kent, not to mention *GMTV* and *The Big Breakfast*.

Chris is 35 and lives in Walthamstowe, North-East London.

Graeme Kay wrote the original edition of the *Coronation Street Quizbook* in 1990. Up until then he had worked for both BBC and ITV in the capacity of television promotions scriptwriter, radio broadcaster, magazine feature writer, and was Senior Press Officer at Granada Television for the three decades. He wrote, "Thousands of us, from journalists and actors to production workers and ancillary staff, have good reason to be grateful to Tony Warren whose creation will have kept us in work for three decades by December this year." Graeme sadly died between the writing and the publication of his book. Both the *Coronation Street Quiz Book* and his other Boxtree book, *Coronation Street 30 Years – 1960 to 1990* remain a testament to the skills and knowledge he acquired over his long career in the television industry.

THE BALDY MAN – CREATING AN IMPRESSION

Colin Gilbert & Niall Clark

* Humour in the tradition of Mr Bean

* Will be shown on television throughout the year

* Hilarious TV show starring Gregor Fisher also known as Rab C Nesbitt

* Baldyman's guide for the reader on how to "make an impression" in modern life

* Unaware of his vanity, bad taste, personal hang-ups and bizarre psychoses, The Baldy Man opens up to the reader giving us what he considers to be honest, good and invaluable advice

* Combined with great photos, capturing all of Gregor's facial grimacing from smug, self satisfied preening to mocking disdain, *Creating an Impression* is set to have the nation rollicking with laughter at The Baldy Man's attempts to be stylish, trendy and cool!

The Baldy Man – Creating An Impression is available from Boxtree, 0 7522 0678 8, priced £7.99 pb

SPECIAL ORDER FORM

BROOKSIDE
1 85283 954 6	Phil Redmond's Brookside: Life in the Close	£9.99 pb
0 7522 0972 8	The Journals of Beth Jordache	£4.99 pb
0 7522 0765 2	Beth Jordache The New Journals	£4.99 pb
0 7522 0846 2	The Jimmy Corkhill Story	£4.99 pb
0 7522 1051 3	The Early Years	£7.99 pb

CORONATION STREET
1 85283 464 1	The Coronation Street Story	£16.99 hb
1 85283 456 0	Life and Times of Rovers Return	£14.99 hb

THE BILL
1 85283 964 3	The Bill: The First Ten Years	£9.99 pb

EMMERDALE
1 85283 959 7	Emmerdale Family Album	£9.99 pb

LONDON'S BURNING
1 85283 874 4	London's Burning	£9.99 pb
0 7522 1085 8	London's Burning: Behind the Blaze	£14.99 hb

SOLDIER, SOLDIER
0 7522 1055 6	Soldier, Soldier – The Regiment Files	£14.99 hb
0 7522 0750 4	Soldier, Soldier Novelisation: Tucker's Story	£4.99 pb
0 7522 0755 5	Soldier, Soldier Novelisation: Damage	£4.99 pb

All these books are available at your local bookshop or can be ordered direct from the publisher. Just tick the titles you want and fill in the form below.

Prices and availability subject to change without notice.

Boxtree Cash Sales, P.O. Box 11, Falmouth, Cornwall TR10 9EN

Please send a cheque or postal order for the value of the book and add the following for postage and packing:

U.K. including B.F.P.O. – £1.00 for one book plus 50p for the second book, and 30p for each additional book ordered up to a £3.00 maximum.

Overseas including Eire – £2.00 for the first book plus £1.00 for the second book, and 50p for each additional book ordered.

OR please debit this amount from my Access/Visa Card (delete as appropriate).

Card Number □□□□□□□□□□□□□□□□□

Amount £ ....

Expiry Date ....

Signed ....

Name ....

Address ....

....

....